I'M STILL YOUR MOTHER

HOW TO GET ALONG WITH YOUR GROWN-UP CHILDREN FOR THE REST OF YOUR LIFE

DR. JANE ADAMS

iUniverse.com, Inc.
San Jose New York Lincoln Shanghai

I'm Still Your Mother
How To Get Along With Your Grown-up Children
For The Rest Of Your Life

Published by iUniverse.com, Inc.

For information address:
iUniverse.com, Inc.
5220 S 16th, Ste. 200
Lincoln, NE 68512
www.iuniverse.com

Originally published by Delacorte

ISBN: 0-595-18358-1

Printed in the United States of America

To Cam and Jenny,
who opened a door in my heart
I never knew was there
and taught me more than I taught them

CONTENTS

INTRODUCTION

COULD THIS BE YOU?

You never worried about an empty nest. All the years they were growing up, you fantasized about what you'd do when they finally did. Turn their rooms into dens, studios, gyms, home offices. Find a full tank of gas in your car, and the radio tuned to golden oldies instead of heavy metal. Keep a quart of Häagen-Dazs in the freezer for more than a day and never discover an empty jar of peanut butter in the back of the cupboard. Take a second honeymoon. Quit, start, or change your job. Sell the house. Buy a condo. Move to Florida. Take a trip on a freighter. Enjoy life—after all, you're entitled.

Your children are gone now, but you're still picking up after them; when you took down the posters and pennants and remodeled his room, you found three plastic retainers he swore were either lost on the bus, eaten by the dog, or fell out of his mouth from the top of the Washington Monument during his class trip.

You still have those raffia table runners your daughter made the summer Herb wanted to air-condition the bedroom but you sent her to Camp Lottadough instead because her best friend was going; the girls stopped speaking to each other the first week, but the mercury didn't get below ninety until Labor Day.

There's still a basketball hoop on the garage door, and when the kids in the neighborhood come over to use it, you don't even mind that endless repetitive thud that once drove you crazy. There are still all those marks on the back of the dining-room door, starting knee high and ending two inches over your head, and you can't bring yourself to paint over them. You have a garage full of sleds, bikes, and racquets and an attic crammed with cribs, clothes, and blocks that you're saving, please God, for the grandchildren. A certificate of appreciation for years of dedicated service as a den mother, and four old cupcake tins and a dozen Star Wars cookie molds. Home movies, scrapbooks, and memories . . . lots of memories.

The days and nights of their childhood are long gone, but the year still starts for you in September and ends in June, and you still wake up at five of seven wondering if they took their lunches. When you hear an ambulance siren in the distance, you do a quick mental inventory—where are the children?—even though your son is climbing a mountain in Nepal and your daughter the lawyer is working herself to death at a big firm three time zones away.

It's just what Herb said when the kids were here for Thanksgiving: By the time they're old enough to be good company, they leave home.

MAYBE THIS IS JUST A STAGE YOU'RE GOING THROUGH

It certainly is, and it's called postparenthood.

Postparenthood starts when the children leave, and lasts until you do. It's the final evolution of your role as a mother and theirs as children, regardless of how old they are or how often you see them.

Dr. Spock never mentioned this stage, and neither do any of the other books. Once you've weathered their adolescence, you're on your own. The assumption is that if you've done your job right, you don't need any advice on how to create and sustain a lively, vibrant, mutual, and affectionate relationship with your adult children.

But that's not so. Being a postparent requires a different set of skills, new rules for new roles. It requires a delicate balance between letting go and holding on, a careful calibration of acknowledgment and inclusion. Because even if your kids are out of your house, they're still in your heart, and they always will be.

What all those other books never told you is that these can be the best years of your life with your children. That this can be the time when all your sacrifice, hard work, and love pay off. When you and they can finally be friends. People who would like each other even if they weren't related. Who would call each other just to talk, even when it wasn't somebody's birthday or a major holiday. Who would be there for each other in good times and bad. Who would stay close even if distance separates you, connected by bonds of love, not guilt or duty. Who would link each other to the past and the future, which is the real meaning of family, and the closest we get to immortality.

IS THIS BOOK FOR YOU?

This book is for you if you want to stay in their lives—and what mother doesn't?

If you raised your kids to be independent, self-reliant,

and think for themselves—and now you lie awake nights worrying while they're doing it.

If you're watching them make decisions about jobs, careers, houses, spouses, children, money, and lifestyle, and wondering if they're making the right ones. If you're hurt because they don't ask your advice, and not sure what to tell them—or how—if they do. If you've never considered asking for theirs, which is too bad, because nobody but a grown son will keep a car salesman from talking you into a sports car, and only an adult daughter can tell you your skirts are too short.

This book is for you if you want to get the most out of the payoff years—if you want to keep your grown children in your life in ways that can nurture and sustain you for years to come.

There may be serious problems in their lives—and yours—that stand in the way of a truly equal and mutual relationship. Many of us, these days, are dealing with more than just the normal friction that ensues when parents and adult children change their accustomed roles and relationships. You may be coping with the fallout from your family's very troubled past, or with present difficulties in your children's lives such as substance abuse or mental or physical illness. If so, there are resources available for more specialized help and support, which are listed at the end of this book. Meanwhile there is plenty in the next nine chapters that applies to all families who are trying to build a happier future together.

YOU'RE STILL THEIR MOTHER

When my son was a baby, I noted each new accomplishment with pride and preserved it for posterity in his baby book, on Super 8 and Kodachrome. And then I rushed to the phone to share the news with my mother.

The first word he ever said was *no,* but she wasn't as thrilled as I was. "You were like that, too," she said. "You always gave me an argument."

Yes, and I never won. Well, hardly ever. I might have consensus, facts, and reason on my side, but it didn't matter. She had the last word . . . the last four words actually.

She never stopped saying them, no matter how old I was. Years after I was an adult—a grandmother in fact—I went to visit her in Florida. We went out for lunch, and when we ordered our meal, she not only told the waiter to make sure there was no sesame oil in the salad dressing, but also repeated the whole story of how I almost died from teething on a sesame bagel when I was a baby. I squirmed in embarrassment, but my mother was not to be quieted. "Would you rather turn blue and choke and go into shock and have to be rushed to the hospital just because they put sesame oil in the salad dressing? You're all grown up now, a big shot, but just remember—" Before she could finish her sentence, four blue-rinsed ladies at the adjoining table did it for her: **"She's still your mother,"** they chanted.

With my own children I vowed I'd never stoop that low. I would convince them of the rightness of my position with facts, statistics, expert opinion—all the things that never worked with my mother. But I soon learned that "I'm still your mother," along with that other great non sequitur "Because I said so," was as necessary to successful child raising as Dr. Spock. It was a powerful, almost mythic incantation. It could stop arguments, quell minor rebellions, and even make them stop whining and pleading. And if it didn't work, you could always give in, which is how my son finally got a dog and my daughter had her ears pierced. (I was the one who had to take the dog out when it rained, and the next thing I knew she had a nose ring, but don't get me started.)

"Because I said so" loses its magic as soon as they realize you're not going to cut them off at the knees, but **"I'm still your mother"** lasts a lifetime—yours, not theirs. Once they're grown up, they may not want to hear it, but that doesn't mean it's not still true. You will be their mother as long as you live. And if you follow the common-sense, time-tested advice in this book, which covers the topics that often provoke conflict between generations but can also be the source of great pride, satisfaction, and delight, they'll want you to be. Because no matter how independent they are, they need you. And no matter how independent you are, you need them too.

CHAPTER ONE

IT AIN'T OVER TILL IT'S OVER

I sat on a park bench catching the late-afternoon sun on a crisp fall day two years ago, hearing but not really listening as three young mothers earnestly discussed pacifiers, preschools, toilet training, and how to tell the mother of the four-year-old bully that her child really needed professional help—topics that have, blissfully, faded from my memory. I remembered days like this one, more than two decades ago, days when the sunshine and sandbox were only a pretext for my real agenda—the company of other

1

women who were dealing with problems like mine, coping with the same issues, and sharing the same experiences. We were our own support group, long before that concept was fashionable; we laughed, we cried, we compared and commiserated, and then, as our kids grew older, we drifted apart. Occasionally I'd run into one of them in the supermarket or the library or at a cocktail party; we'd bring each other up-to-date on our lives, pull out the snapshots in our wallets, brag about how well our kids were doing, or lie about it if they weren't.

I thought that day in the park about the fact that I hardly ever talked to anyone anymore about my children. Oh, I still showed the pictures, gave the vital statistics, and bragged or lied as appropriate. But it was all surface stuff—not the real feelings I had when she brought home her future husband and I absolutely knew it was a mistake, or he dropped out of school and into the Help Wanteds without a degree or credential in anything except maybe Advanced Ski Bum, and I wondered what would ever become of him. They were grown (nearly) and gone (mostly), and although I thought about them often and worried about them occasionally, I was supposed to be beyond all that. To do otherwise—to dwell on or even mention my concerns about them, or my confusion about who I was now that the key role by which I had identified myself for so many years no longer fit—was, I assumed, to invite scorn, and even pity. "Poor thing," I could imagine people saying, "she just can't let go."

2

Since I have made a career of finding out and writing about how other women are dealing with whatever life stage I happen to be experiencing, I started keeping a file marked NLG (Not Letting Go).

That was the beginning of this book—that and the evening that followed a few weeks later, when I looked up a dozen of the women I used to know when our children were in the same preschool or car pool or Little League, and put them together to talk about what it's like to be what Peggy, who was my best friend then and still is, calls Zombie Mothers.

We talked long into the night, consumed many bottles of wine, shared our fears and our pains and our prides and joys, laughed till we cried and cried till we had to laugh. It was a high-estrogen event, a cross between a CR group and a twelve-step meeting. Here are some of the things we said:

"I feel as if I've been struggling with some of these issues and worries all by myself, and now that I know I'm not the only one, I feel a lot better."

"The worst thing is when friends whose kids are doing fine, or who don't have kids at all, tell me not to feel what I'm feeling. They call me codependent. Well, I remember when that was a good definition of being a mother!"

"We're not supposed to worry, we're not supposed to feel guilty or responsible, and we're not supposed to talk about the grandchildren. Now, in all your life you never saw such beautiful kids. . . ."

3

THE SILENT MINORITY: ISN'T HE STILL THEIR FATHER TOO?

You may wonder where our children's fathers are, at least in the pages of this book. Did all of us bring up our kids alone, or are we coping with postparenthood by ourselves?

Not at all. I interviewed close to a hundred mothers, and in a number of instances their husbands were also present . . . sort of. They were watching Monday-night football in the den while we were talking in the kitchen. During halftime they often wandered in and shared their wisdom and concerns. But I wanted to describe as well as prescribe—to focus on the emotional as well as the practical aspects of postparenthood, on how it feels to *be* at this life stage as well as what to *do* about it. And since men of our generation are still not comfortable talking about their feelings, their wives often did or do it for them.

Also, in keeping with the statistical norms for this generation, over half of the women I interviewed were or are divorced, which is why it may sometimes sound like this is a book about single postparents. It isn't. While you may not hear fathers' voices as clearly or as often in these pages as you do mothers', it's not because they couldn't get a word in edgewise or didn't have anything to say. They could and they did, and some of the most sensible advice herein is theirs.

A note about who the voices in this and the following chapters belong to: Because so many people participated, identifying them individually proved cumbersome. Also a significant number of those I interviewed were concerned about protecting their children's privacy. I wanted to honor that confidentiality and also to include as many different voices as possible, so rather than create composites, which blur authenticity, I chose instead to set their remarks off in italics. But it is important to understand who these people are—to describe the sample, as sociologists say—and indicate what, besides grown kids, we have in common.

POSTPARENTS—WHO WE ARE

Our offspring range in age from twenty to thirty-five. We live in cities and suburbs, are mostly college educated, and predominately middle-class, although that classification, economically at least, stretches from just getting by to quite comfortable, thank you. Eighty percent of us are white, 20 percent black, Asian, and Hispanic, and most of us are in our fifties. All but a handful work outside the home, though many of us didn't join the labor force until our kids were in school, and those who don't have paid jobs now are active community volunteers or are enrolled in academic programs.

We are a generation on the cusp—as Barbara Raskin

said in her novel *Hot Flashes*, we were the last women to get dressed up to go to the airport. We came to adulthood between the mid-fifties and early sixties and were just settling into our grown-up lives by the time the great social upheavals of the past quarter century occurred. The defining ideologies of that period—especially feminism, the sexual revolution, and the human-potential movement—changed our lives in ways we could not have imagined.

We never expected to have to support ourselves, but we were propelled by need or desire into the job market. We married in our early twenties, but a number of us were divorced because we grew in different directions, or we needed our own space, or he did—it's been so long we can't remember. We had little or no sexual experience before marriage and assumed we'd have only one, lifetime sexual partner, but if we divorced, we had more of those than we care to remember now, and if we didn't, we're slightly envious of those who did (not enough to leave our husbands, though). We are the children of parents who lived through the Great Depression and a world war and who raised us with the assurance that if we worked hard, got a decent education and a steady job, and followed the rules, our lives would turn out okay.

That nebulous concept "happiness" was not in our parents' vocabulary—security was the goal that was held out to us. "Whoever said you're supposed to be happy?" is a refrain most of us heard over and over again while we were growing up. And while the values, morals, and attitudes of the society in which we were raising our children were turned upside down, even the most traditional and conser- - vative among us began to answer that refrain with a question of our own: "Who says you're not?"

WHAT WE WANT FOR OUR CHILDREN

The first key finding that emerged from all of the interviews I conducted delineates a value shift that has occurred in a generation poised midway between two very different lifestyles: While financial security, marital stability, and career achievement were the primary goals our parents had for us, what we want most for our children is the fulfillment of their personal, individual potential, which is what *we* call happiness.

Believing initially that this slightly New Age concept was a West Coast phenomenon, I expanded my interviewing to include a more geographically and culturally diverse population—women who think a channeler is what you use to switch TV stations, who remember Shirley MacLaine when she only had one life, who'd never have been caught dead in an encounter group. But although the words varied—*self-esteem, satisfaction, feeling okay about oneself, being comfortable in one's own skin, being in touch with one's feelings, being centered*—the meaning was clear.

"My mother used to say, 'I don't care what you do as long as you're happy.' But what she really meant was, 'Marry a man with a good job, get a teaching degree so you'll always have something to fall back on if he gets sick or dies, keep your figure so he won't leave you, and never buy anything on credit.' But security is an illusion. In the end the only thing you really have to fall back on is yourself. And that's what I want for my kids—to know themselves and be happy with who they are. All the rest is bullshit. But they are much more realistic than I was. My daughter said to me, 'I wish you'd just told me to be a concert pianist or the first woman president. That would be a lot easier than being happy.'

"I don't want my kids to feel driven, the way I was, herded into a life I have mapped out for them. My parents wanted to narrow the world for me, to make it safe—I want to widen it for my children."

"I don't feel I had many choices, because of the era I grew up in. The older I get, the more I realize how the fifties hemmed me in. We see the emptiness of the promise our parents held out to us, and we know there's a better way, we just don't know exactly what it is. I love their freedom to invent lives that please them, to be happy in their own way, but I also worry about those other things, like getting their college degrees and being able to support themselves, all these old messages from my upbringing about the 'right' way to live. We swallowed, hook, line, and sinker, what our *parents told us, and we still have a lot of it in us, but we also want our kids to be happy in their own ways—it's our internal struggle that our kids see and are confused by. It's our job to figure out the struggle so that we can be authentic about supporting them, realizing that they're going to make choices that are very different from ours, but boy, is it hard!"*

That comment sums up the bind we fifty-somethings find ourselves in—the conflicting goals we have for our children. But it also highlights the surprising degree of confidence most of us feel in their ability to figure it out for themselves.

"Our kids aren't driven the way we were; if the future isn't laid out so clearly for them, they are going to be—they are—a lot more thoughtful and know themselves better than we did. I trust them to make good decisions, decisions that will really make a difference in the quality of their lives, the happiness they find, in ways my parents didn't trust me."

WHAT WE WANT FOR OURSELVES

The second key finding is that what we want for ourselves is something most of us don't feel we had with our mothers: an honest, intimate, authentic, and egalitarian relationship with our adult children.

"I would never have told my mother she pissed me off, even when she did, which was a lot. She criticizes the way

my kids have always talked back and questioned me, which they still do, even though they're grown now. But we are much more equal than my parents and I were and as a result much closer. I would say I had a pretty good relationship with my mother, but I wouldn't call it a real one—that quality of honesty I have with my kids was never there. I've told my kids I never want them to see me because they feel obligated to—only because they love me and want to be with me. I would never make them feel guilty about being caught up in their own lives the way my mother does. But then I have a life of my own, which she didn't have after we left. Lots of times I'm not even around when my kids want to see me. I think that's my greatest achievement as a parent— being someone my grown kids enjoy."

"The way my mother felt about wanting me to have a more comfortable life than she had is the way I feel about wanting a real relationship with my daughter. I don't think my kids will have a better life in material terms than I do— in fact they may not even have one as comfortable as mine. I can't do anything about that—it's the economy, it's the world, the fact that we were raised in a time of surplus and our kids have to learn to live with less. What I can do something about is the quality of how we are together as human beings. What has changed since my mother's day is not just the outer world but the inner one—what we expect out of all our relationships, including the one with our grown kids."

WHY WE ARE WORRIED NOW

The third key finding is this: We are less certain of our ability to be good role models for our children now than at any other stage in their development, and this is directly related to our feeling that we are not yet fully mature ourselves.

"Rightly or wrongly, I think my parents had stopped growing by the time they were the age I am now. They were not as self-conscious as we are, and more frightened of change. Now we see personal growth as a lifelong process, which means that we see ourselves as still evolving. I mean, if you're having your own midlife crisis, reexamining things all the time, how can you be this wellspring of wisdom and certainty for your kids?"

"The world is so different from when I was growing up. I don't know diddly squat about their world. I feel bad about what they're facing, but I don't have a clue, and I hope they do. I can say, here's how I did it, but I don't know that it's at all relevant. Our parents thought their advice was relevant, but I know better. Whatever expectations I had for my kids are gone now, because my own life is so different from how I expected it to be. For one thing I thought that by the time I hit fifty, I'd know all the answers. And guess what? I don't even know the questions!"

"If my parents ever had a midlife crisis, they kept it to themselves. Because of our more open relationship with

11

our kids, they are more aware of our uncertainties than we were of our parents'. When they ask, 'What am I going to do with my life?' all I can say is, 'How should I know, when I don't know what I'm going to do with my own?' "

As Susan Littwin points out in *The Postponed Generation,* today's children are growing up almost a decade later than we did. So it may be that their delayed maturity has delayed ours as well. Or perhaps we used to think that when we got to the half-century mark, who we were would be fixed like a fly in amber. But the relatively recent emphasis on growth as a lifelong process—the emergence of adult development as a major field of research and the popularization of its primary theorists such as Roger Gould, Gail Sheehy, Daniel Levinson, and others—has changed our perception of what maturity is. Middle age may now start at 55 and last until we get our senior-citizen discount cards, but as Johnny Carson pointed out, he doesn't know many 110-year-olds.

How close we are to our goals—for our children and for ourselves—determines the emotional affect of being post-parents. And how we feel about them and ourselves at this stage of our lives and theirs is determined by the following factors:

- How our children are actually doing with their lives

- How well we feel we mothered them

- Whether we raised them alone or with a partner

- What our expectations of them were

- What we think our relationship with them should be

- What our relationship with them actually is

CORE IDENTITIES AND SHIFTING ROLES

We fifty-somethings have worked outside the home during some or all of our children's youth. Most of our mothers were only mothers, and when we left, it was the end of their job. When our children left, we still had jobs, other roles, other aspects of our selves we wanted to explore. So it has come as a rueful surprise to those of us who thought we couldn't wait for an empty nest that whatever else we have done with our lives, our longest role and responsibility has been as mothers. Motherhood is a fixed, embedded aspect of self that remains as a core identity for all of us. Despite our multifarious roles, it would be among the top three descriptors, regardless of who else we are, how old our kids are, how far away they live, or even how close to or estranged from them we may be. Women are relational beings, as Carol Gilligan has pointed out, and we constellate our personal world accordingly. Says a woman who is, among other things, a judge, wife, artist, athlete, and writer, *"If I couldn't say I did okay as a mom and I'm doing okay as one now, it would be unimaginably painful—what I want it to say on my tombstone is, 'She was a great mother.' "*

13

When we talked that first night about what still being their mother meant, the general consensus was that at this stage of our children's lives motherhood is an identity that is more emotive than affective; in other words we feel that way more than we act that way. Except in times of crisis we are not their caretakers anymore, but we still think we should be: *"If they're not happy, I get the feeling I should be doing something for them, taking over for them."*

"I'm still your mother—aren't I?" is a plaintive cry, whether or not we actually utter it, when we feel our children are distancing themselves from us: *"That's what I think with my older daughter, who's very critical and who I always feel wants to break up with me."*

And it's a sigh of resignation when we wish they were more independent: *"When my thirty-year-old can't balance her budget and needs to cover the rent, I think, well, I'm still her mother."*

It's the excuse we give ourselves for transgressing their personal boundaries, taking liberties with them that we would not take with anyone else, whether it's criticizing their lifestyles, straightening his tie, or pushing the hair out of her eyes. *"I don't think they've had as much problem individuating from me as I have individuating from them. My struggle is to not tell her she's gained weight, or to not clean his apartment when I visit."*

It's why we feel their pain and joy. *"I'm still their*

mother because I haven't disburdened myself of carrying their events in me psychically; when she was pregnant, I even had nightmares about giving birth myself, because I know she's not cooked enough psychologically to have a child—I assume the burden of their choices in my heart, even though I'd like not to. I'd like to be on the other side of that great divide."

It's not our only role or identity, but for most of us it is the one immutable, unchangeable, lifelong one. *"It doesn't matter how old they are or I am, I'm still their mother, and I care about them and their welfare just as much and just as deeply as I once did. Well, maybe not quite as deeply. When they were little and had to have shots, I used to tell them it hurt me more than it hurt them. And when they were older—when my daughter was treated badly by a boyfriend, when my son didn't make the team, I think I suffered their pain longer and deeper than they did. But now when they hurt, it's like the memory of pain, not the pain itself."*

Still being their mother, she added, means her heart is connected to her children in such a way that it will sing or cry, depending on them. Like most of us she is trying to figure out the appropriate place for her to be, the right distance. This is still a developmental stage, for her as well as for them, but there are no guidelines for her.

HOW THEY'RE DOING

Most of our children are doing okay, though the path to their maturity has been circuitous and marked by deviations from the more-or-less straight lines we followed. Those who went to college took much longer to finish than we did. My own son used to have a T-shirt from his college that proclaimed "Five or Six of the Best Years of Your Life," and his was not an atypical course. Many children had considerable experience with substances that weren't even in our vocabulary, and although most came out of that experimentation without long-lasting damage, a few were seriously harmed by drug and alcohol abuse. Most of our children have had multiple romantic and sexual partners, and we pride ourselves on being much more accepting of this than our own parents might have been—had they known. Some of our sons and daughters are gay, and all of us have gone through predictable stages of worry, grief, and, finally, acceptance of their sexual identity. Still, we would rather know than not know. *"I have a brother who's gay who was in the closet all his life, until my parents died, and I would never want that shame and secrecy for my son,"* said the mother of a young man who came out to his parents when he was nineteen.

Our children are having greater financial and economic struggles than we did, and yet they are a generation who feel entitled to material comforts, often all out of proportion to what we expected at their age. Over 35 percent of those between eighteen and twenty-five and 12 percent of those between twenty-five and thirty-four are still living at home or have returned there; the boomerang phenomenon has come home to many of us, with not altogether satisfying results: *"I was so eager to get out of my mother's house, I didn't care where or how I lived. But my son, who has a low-paying job, is used to a higher level of comfort. Unfortunately the only place he can get it is back home."*

To a woman, everyone I spoke with expressed surprise and some dismay about the fact that most of our children seem to be taking so long to grow up, at least by conventional measurements. The rituals that once marked adulthood—graduation, the first job, marriage, children— have been delayed, eliminated, or extended. To many of us this is a mixed blessing. On the one hand we don't want them to limit their options; on the other there are so many more options available to them than we think were open to us: *"I don't want him to wake up at forty and say, 'I never really did what I wanted,' the way his father did. But he's twenty-six, and part of me wants to see him settled down."*

A woman who married at twenty-two and divorced ten years later told her daughter that if she got married before she was thirty, she'd nail her foot to the floor: *"But in this age of AIDS, I don't want a sexually active twenty-two-year-old, either, and I find myself hoping she'll marry her boyfriend, even though I'm not sure he's the right man for her."*

Someone else's oldest daughter is twenty-six and still lives at home: *"Not only is she in no hurry to leave, but her father doesn't want her to either. He was away a great deal when she was little, and he likes getting to know her now. And I enjoy her tremendously. But I realize that none of us, including her, will take her seriously as an adult until she does, until she's responsible for herself. By letting her stay, are we contributing to her arrested development?"*

We are of mixed minds about the prolonged young adulthood that marks our kids' generation. Some of us regret that we were not able to provide them with the secure childhood our parents gave us, particularly those of us who were divorced during their younger years. But we also believe, as Susan Littwin points out, that *"they have their own truly special if not eccentric kind of strength precisely because of the history that gave them their vulnerabilities. They deal with uncertainty and ambivalence better than we do because they have had more practice. They have a greater capacity to enjoy life because they have had so much more practice. As a generation they may have more talent for recreation than any in history, which gives them great resilience and an ability to set aside for a while problems that might ravage their parents. So even their escapism has its value. Most of all their sense of specialness gives them a hidden layer of ego strength. They may crack or run away when the world does not treat them as they expect, but they are not done for. That sense of their own worth—no matter how tattered it may be—enables them to rebound and grow up . . . just a little later."*

HOW WE'RE DOING

While how we feel has something to do with what shape our kids are in, our own judgments about our performance as mothers has much greater influence on our level of self-satisfaction today. *"Maybe if I felt better about how I was when they were growing up, I'd feel less anxious about losing their love now,"* said a woman who spent much of their childhood intensely involved in the politics of the women's movement.

"I was so busy when he was little creating a life, a person, I wasn't really his mother, even though I was there. I have more regrets now that he's grown and gone. I long for him to live nearer me so I can do for him now what I didn't do then, and sorry that he doesn't need me to," said a therapist who finished college, graduate school, and established a practice when her son was young.

And another woman, who was divorced when her daughter was three, reported, *"I really didn't give her the kind of mothering I should have, maybe because I was so involved in trying to find her a father. I feel more into being a mother now, being the person she can turn to, who'll always be there for her. When she's in trouble, there's part of me that's in trouble, and now I can acknowledge it and help without feeling like somehow it's my fault, or be personally threatened by it."*

The phrase *doing it right* came up again and again, perhaps because we are a generation of overachievers. *"I keep trying to do it right—that's why I had a baby at forty-four, when my oldest was twenty. I think, this time I know so much more, I'm so much more aware, so much more capable. And now he's ten, and I am better with him than I was with the others, but I still have guilt—can you be a mother without having guilt?"*

It's hard to feel like we did it right when our children have serious problems: *"I finally think I was a good enough mother, even though one of my kids had a major problem with alcohol and the other, at twenty-eight, still hasn't found himself, whatever that means. Of course it's taken four years of analysis and fifty thousand dollars for me to get to that point."*

What we all agreed on was that we'd done the best we could, given who we were and, even more important, who they were. *"For all the nature/nurture controversy that, during the years my kids were growing up, was heavily biased in favor of nurture being the big determinant, my kids came into this world with certain givens that I couldn't do anything about, nor could they. I did better with Tory and Jason, because they were more like me—but with Andrea it was tough sledding from the beginning. She challenged me from the day she was born, demanded more of me, required wisdom or patience or something I just didn't have then."*

More than any other factor—age, race, social or economic class—whether we raised them alone or with their father influences the level of satisfaction most women feel about themselves as mothers, both in the past and presently. Surprisingly it seems to have little correlation with how well our children are doing. There is a universal feeling among single mothers that they put undue burdens on their kids by sharing too much of themselves with them—that they were inappropriately meshed, that they robbed them of the innocence of childhood, that they were too busy trying to figure out their own lives to parent them properly. *"I always felt I was a good mother to my daughter—I gave her everything I could. So when she said to me recently, I feel like lots of times I was the mother, I felt really guilty, like I failed in the deepest way, because I didn't give her a father."*

Single mothers remain less secure than intact families about our connection with our children: *"I always worry that she won't love me, and as a divorced mother that makes me feel very alone."* And most of us who were or are single mothers agreed that we always did and still do connect whatever problems our kids had then or now to the effect on them of our divorces. But we also feel a great sense of pride in what we did accomplish, and when we listen to other women talk about their experiences in trying to reconcile

21

two different ways of doing and being parents, we feel relieved that we didn't have to compromise our own parenting beliefs or principles with someone else's.

We don't feel that our mothers' experiences offer useful guidelines for the more authentic relationships we want with our children, or for giving them the support and uncritical acceptance we think will further their chance to be happy. And to a certain extent we are right, although, as one woman put it, *"I have not been as demanding of my daughter as my mother was with me, which may be why we have a better relationship. Yet as I get older, I begin to wonder if maybe I shouldn't have been so all-accepting—if that was the right thing for her, even though it seemed like the right thing for us."*

For all that we think of ourselves as pioneers, perhaps that is only generational hubris and we will get our comeuppance when our children are seeing theirs off to adulthood and feeling the same way we do now.

But of one thing we are confident: Neither the quality of authentic intimacy we say we want with them nor the personal satisfactions and emotional security we want for them is possible until we have dealt honestly and openly with whatever unfinished business is left between us.

CHAPTER TWO

FINISHING UP YOUR BUSINESS WITH YOUR KIDS

"Are we having a Princess attack?" asked my son. It was dawn on the Dark Continent, and as I struggled out of my sleeping bag, slapping at mosquitoes, I felt every muscle protest yesterday's long, jouncing journey in the Land Rover and last night's restless sleep with only a few inches of foam rubber separating my body from the Serengetti's unforgiving contours. Adventure travel, they call it, but as I sipped the hot coffee he handed me, I reflected that this was the real adventure—not Africa but us, he and I. We had arrived, finally, at a destination only dimly glimpsed during all the difficult years that preceded this one. At twenty he was an Almost Adult, and I a Postparent—and this was the place marked Payoff Years on the map that every mother carries in her heart.

It was not always thus. We nearly lost each other during that awful time of surging hormones and daily defiance one of the countless experts I consulted back then called nature's own psychosis. At fourteen he went to live with his father. Letting go was complicated by guilt, hurt, and anger, but of course it was only practice for the harder task, the one that awaits every parent someday—letting go for good. Before that day occurred, I wanted to repair our ravaged relationship, make friends and amends. Postparenting, I hoped, was the time that could happen, the window of opportunity when kids are grown but not gone, out of our homes but not out of our hearts or lives. Postparenting is about creating new relationships with nearly grown children—seeing them off, hoping they make it, and being there with a safety net. Most of all it's about making a family strong even as external forces— distance, autonomy, and different priorities—tug on the ties that bind.

It is a challenge to have a vibrant relationship with adult children, Harvard educator and psychiatrist Robert Kegan, author of *The Evolving Self,* a neo-Piagetian approach to personality psychology, told me—a challenge, but not impossible, even if getting from there to here was difficult and left scars on everyone. In the effort not to repeat the mistakes our parents made, said Dr. Kegan, we often do the opposite with our own offspring. My mother never acknowledged me as separate from her; I never had a self she didn't have a lien on. I carried into adulthood her compromised message: "Go if you must, but if you do, I'll die." Long after I was grown, I felt that I was only pretending to be an adult. I fought continuously to maintain my distance from her, went to the opposite end of the continent in fact and remained there, reconnecting only when I was hurt, broke, or in trouble.

With my son, I vowed, I'd never do that. And when he became a surly, alienated teenager, I did the distancing before he could. I couldn't accept the person he seemed bent on becoming, couldn't tolerate his choices about goals, values, friends. It wasn't the hair or the clothes or the music, it was the either-orness of adolescence that defeated me. The apathy or anger, the cruelty or kindness, the brilliance or stupidity, the love or hate. I was exhausted from wondering who would (or wouldn't) appear at the breakfast table. Establishing real, physical boundaries between us was necessary for his own good, I told myself, but actually it was for mine as well; if I could not separate from him emotionally, I would never feel whole when being a mother was no longer a full-time job, and he would make demands on me for the rest of our lives. As a postparent, says Dr. Kegan, one must learn to touch without grasping—a difficult but valuable skill, one that teaches that when you are gone, they will be able to go on. And that realization can free you both to live and love on your own terms of endearment.

The end of adolescence is a dynamic moment in emotional growth—ours as well as theirs. While they're leaving home, we're letting go. Our development as postparents is roughly equivalent to theirs as adults. It's a process that begins when they're around eighteen and lasts until a new equilibrium is established. Because it's a process rather than a single event, it can be influenced with appropriate intervention. What Dr. Kegan calls faulty loving in the family of origin is the key to reconstructing a healthier relationship with a nearly grown child. Faulty loving is the failure either to acknowledge or to include. The first starts early, when we have difficulty accepting kids as separate from ourselves, acknowledging their selfhood and individuality. The second often surfaces during adolescence, when we respond to the choices they have made by separating ourselves from them. The nonacknowledging parent wonders why a child can't seem to grow up, unaware that she won't let him; the nonincluding parent wonders what happened to her sweet, tractable daughter, or who that careless, unkempt, angry boy sulking in his room could be and distances herself emotionally from this sudden stranger.

So, effective postparenting requires a clear-eyed analysis of the relationship we've had with our kids and a determination to reverse course, to do the opposite. If we've never been able to see them as separate beings, advises Dr. Kegan, this is the time to do so. To listen, not judge. To hear who they've become and hope we can live with it. To establish our boundaries and accept theirs. Inclusion is trickier, especially if death, divorce, or remarriage has altered the family unit they grew up in. What's called for are words and actions that remind them that we value them, that we cherish our shared history and recognize the mutual need for connection and intimacy even as we live our separate lives. Just as acknowledging is about establishing boundaries, including may be about letting some down.

In Africa with my son I had a chance to test Dr. Kegan's ideas about postparenting. On this trip, I hoped, we might both have a chance to experience ourselves differently—not as parent and child but as near equals, part of a group that didn't know our troubled history together, only that we, like they, had a taste for exotic travel, new people and places, and a longtime fascination with Africa. I had the money and he had the time, and we both had trepidations. Mine had to do with whether I could cope with the demands five weeks of rugged travel would make on my middle-aged body. His were about being the youngest person in our group of eight, being infantilized by my presence. We didn't talk about our other fears until much later—on the plane home, when he said, "I know this sounds weird, Mom, but I'll remember you and me on this trip even when you're dead."

Of course that was what it was all about, although I didn't realize it at the time. Letting go and holding on, both at the same time—is it possible? Postparenting means giving up control—or the illusion that we ever had it. It means giving up responsibility, too—oh, blessed relief. And most of all guilt—that has to be the first thing to go. We do the best we can as parents, and most of our mistakes result from loving too much rather than too little. Halfway around the world I realized that it isn't over till it's over—and if we're lucky, it may not even be over then.

IF WE HAD IT TO DO OVER AGAIN, WE WOULDN'T

To those of you who picked up this book remembering and regretting all the mistakes you made while raising your children and hoped to find in it a magic formula to replace the imperfect, overburdened, unprepared, and unaware parent you think you were with the wise, loving, temperate, conscious, perfect one you'd be if only you had a second chance, I have some good news and some bad news.

First the bad news. You won't have a second chance unless your stretch marks are as faint as your memory and you're ready to mix formula in the middle of the night again.

And now the good news. Even if you weren't June Cleaver or Maria Von Trapp back then, you can still qualify for the finals.

Of course maybe you were a supermother who never said an insensitive thing to your child, never stepped on his or her feelings, boundaries, dreams, or desires, never guilt-checked or power-tripped. Perhaps you were so secure and content in your life, your marriage, and your relationship with your own parents that you not only managed to avoid repeating the mistakes they made but didn't make any others either. You may never have had difficulties balancing your needs with theirs or effortlessly juggling your roles as wife, mother, and human being. You might even have stayed true to your values and exemplified them consistently for your children while the turbulent sixties and seventies were turning values upside down for the entire culture.

If so, you probably don't need to read this chapter now. Save it till he or she goes into therapy, or needs someone to blame for the fact that life didn't turn out to be problem-free.

But for the rest of us, the time to finish up our business with our children is right now.

Why bother? Why put ourselves through unnecessary pain? After all, the past can't be changed, so why dredge it up? *"Why should I risk the relationship I have with her now, distant and dissatisfying as it sometimes is, for something that could get a lot worse before it gets better? Or maybe even not get any better at all?"*

SOONER, NOT LATER

For one thing, life is unpredictable. Any one of us could get hit by a Mack truck tomorrow and miss the chance. For another, if we keep putting it off, it'll never happen, because our kids will get on with their lives without us. They'll come to terms with the past in whatever way allows them to live most comfortably in the present. That may mean anything from cutting off communication entirely to continuing to see and relate to us in ways that don't have anything to do with the person we are now, and may not even bear much resemblance to who we were then.

It doesn't matter. Dr. Kegan describes the "zone of mediation where meaning is made—the region between an event and the reaction to it" as the place where an event is privately composed, made personal sense of; the place and the way a person holds himself together. In that zone our children have made their own meaning of their experience, and we can't change it. All we can do is listen to it, acknowledge it, and, most important, accept it as being true for them.

"I think her inability to get her life started has some-

thing to do with how she felt growing up, and that she blames me for it, but I can never get her to articulate what it is. I mean, what's the indictment? What did I do?" asks a woman who suspects, as do those of us who see our children still floundering in many ways, that unfinished business in the past may be keeping her grown child from living successfully in the present. If they are stumbling in their efforts to function fully as adults, is there anything we can do, short of outright rescue, to help? Or would we just be undercutting their independence, postponing the moment when they will have to live their own lives, solve their own problems?

Roger Gould, a pioneer in the field of adult development, points out that the illusion that life pays off automatically is supported by a combination of seductive social myths and the desire to live in a pain-free state. In order for our children to challenge this assumption successfully, we must resist the tendency to rescue them. Only when the assumption is finally rejected are they free to modify or reject the initial choices made in their late teens and early twenties, to revise their childhood expectations that our way of living, doing, and being is the only way. But between the challenge and the rejection is a period of time when their independence is still too shaky to admit or even acknowledge to themselves their need for our love and validation, which is stronger in early adulthood than at any time since very early childhood. So they may be focusing on earlier times when they needed us in different ways and, for one reason or another, we failed them. Their need may be submerged under layers of blame and anger—and so may our guilt.

MOTHER'S GUILT IS NEVER DONE

"Until a couple of years ago, she was very clingy, not dependent financially, but wanting me to make her decisions for her. Then she just cut me out of her life entirely. She married someone she'd only known for a month and moved to Hawaii with him. It didn't work out, and she came back, but she was back for two months before she even called me. And when she did, she was very angry. She finally agreed to go into counseling, and her therapist suggested I come in for a session. It was the worst hour of my life. I just sat there while she dumped all her resentments on me, and I cried for a week after that. I went twice more, and then I said, 'Enough, I'm not paying a hundred dollars an hour for you to blame everything on me.' And then the therapist said, 'Oh, good—finally. Now we can get started.' And after that, it was easier. I even said to her, 'You're my daughter. I'm still your mother. It's not like I'm a boyfriend you can break up with. We're stuck with each other, and we're just going to have to work it out.' "

Guilt is a hot potato parents and their offspring toss

around throughout their lives. But somehow it always lands in the laps of mothers. When it comes to taking the blame, we are the Chosen. What shrinks and society don't heap on us we are all too eager to take on ourselves. Mother bashing is both a spectator and a participant sport. It takes different labels in different times. Philip Wylie blamed the evils of the postwar world on momism. Today it's called codependency, a concept useful in the understanding and treatment of addiction but way too simplistic, most of us believe, to describe a relationship that by its very nature is one-sided—at least for the first twenty years or so. As Paula Kaplan points out in *Don't Blame Mother,* therapists are quick to blame us for whatever went wrong in our children's developing psyches; fathers, unless abusers or alcoholics, usually get off scot-free.

Nobody gets through childhood without a mark on them. The "dysfunctional family" is almost a cliché by now, a catchall label applied to many circumstances in which it's neither clinically warranted nor psychologically valid. It surprises and dismays us when our grown child sticks it to us, and if he or she does so on prime-time television or in the pages of a best-selling book, as is increasingly common, even Nancy Reagan evokes our sympathies. The fact is that few families manage to answer all of the needs of all their members all the time, and ours was probably no exception—neither the one we were born into nor the one we created with our children.

IT'S THEIR STORY, AND THEY'RE STICKING TO IT

There are parents who failed their children in deep and significant ways, and they feel their guilt intensely. *Abuse* is one of the labels we attach to such failures, but, like *dysfunctional,* it has attracted a grab bag of redefinitions. I am not talking here about sexual or physical abuse, a circumstance whose effects on both parent and child may and probably will require the kind of help only trained professionals can provide. Emotional abuse is something else— like beauty, it's in the eyes of the beholder.

Here is an example of such labeling that seems totally absurd, yet it is by no means extreme or unusual: Dolores's daughter had long, fine, hard-to-manage hair that snarled easily, evoking yelps of pain with every stroke of the brush. "Every morning we went through hell," Dolores remembered. "She ended up in tears, and I was exhausted. So I took her to my hairdresser and had him cut it into a pixie. I thought she looked adorable. Now she says I mutilated her, that she was an abused child. Can you imagine?"

Resisting the labels—*dysfunctional, abusive*—when common sense tells you your family life didn't warrant them is more than simply self-defense; it's necessary in order to avoid allowing your children to identify themselves as victims and thus make you the scapegoat for their problems. But it's also important to remember that much of

34

what is defined today as abuse was simply the norm when we were raised, and some of what we did as parents was an attempt to redress the grievances of our childhood by going to extremes in the other direction. For instance if we came from a controlling, boundary-invading family, we may have overcompensated by being extremely permissive, liberal, and overly respective of boundaries with our children. But what we accomplished in spite of our efforts was to complete the pattern by allowing them to walk all over us. In attempting to do the right thing—the opposite of what our parents did with us—we simply shifted the controlling, abusive authority to our children.

The more difficult it is for our children to make the passage to adulthood, the more we're likely to come in for a major share of the blame. The more we take it, the tougher it will be for them in the long run, because it will rob them of the opportunity to take responsibility for themselves in the lives they're leading now. Maybe, like Rosie, we did stuff food into our daughter's mouth to pacify or reward her when she was a little girl—"Still, it's not my fault that she's twenty pounds overweight today. I haven't been putting food in her mouth for years," Rosie says indignantly. "But as long as I accept the blame, she never has to deny herself a chocolate éclair."

The purpose of blame is to shift responsibility. If we accept it, our children will be trapped in dependency, which will hamper their efforts to stand on their own.

The amount of damage people sustain in childhood depends on other factors besides parents. There may be traumas related to school, peers, siblings, or other circumstances known or unknown to us that affect one child deeply and barely graze the consciousness of another: *"Kids are born into this world hard-wired, and everyone's wiring—their psychic strength or fragility—is different. One of mine was just born an open wound, she feels and hurts and suffers very deeply, and the other always had this inner strength, he's very resilient. It's like one's from the moon and one's from earth—they have totally different recollections of the same event."*

DOES THERAPY MAKE IT BETTER OR WORSE?

Many young adults turn to therapy, or even self-help books, to make sense of their lives during a time as confusing in its way as adolescence was. From Freud to family origin, most therapies trace present conflicts back to their roots in the past. Which means us. No matter what we did, chances are that we are going to take a beating when our kids are on the couch. We hope that by the time they (or we) have paid the last shrink bill, our grown children will have gained enough understanding and compassion to put the past in perspective, to understand that, whatever we did or didn't do, it wasn't because we didn't love them or they weren't lovable.

Young adults in counseling often feel a need to confront their parents about what went on in their family in the past or is even still going on. Other crises or key events in their life may also stimulate their desire to open up their relationship with us to greater scrutiny, and they may do so in an accusatory, blaming fashion. What's important here is their willingness to engage the issue. Even if they don't do it as clearly, politely, or positively as we might wish, the important thing is that they've risked a great deal in doing so. So it's doubly important that we give their grievances a fair airing.

"If you are the one who recognizes that the relationship needs improvement, then the onus is on you to open things up in a way that doesn't put them on the defensive," says Judith Gordon, a family therapist, "but still signals your sincere desire to put the past behind you and create a new and better way of being together." She suggests broaching the subject gently and in a nonthreatening way—a simple statement to the effect that you realize there's something in the way of your having a close, loving connection and that you're willing to work with your child, alone or with others in the family, to find and ameliorate it. If relations have been extremely tense or strained between you, offers Shauna L. Smith, author of *Making Peace with Your Adult Children,* write a letter stating your offer, your interest in finding a neutral time and place to talk, your wish to engage as adults and peers rather than parent and child, your realization that either or both of you may have done things in the past that have contributed to the breakdown, and your genuine regret that this happened.

Many of us have struggled through painful but ultimately positive attempts to heal our relationships with our children. Some of us went into counseling with them, others sought professional help ourselves or with our husbands, and many of us just muddled through. We learned that choosing the time and place is extremely important. To face off in what may be, at least in the beginning, an explosive and confrontational exchange, without any prior warning, or in the midst of an already potentially tense occasion, such as a holiday meal, a family reunion, or a crisis involving other family members, is at best foolhardy, at worst sneaky: *"It took a particularly awful Thanksgiving, when I looked around the table and I saw how far away from me my daughter had deliberately placed herself and realized that she had not spoken one word to me the whole afternoon—not one actual word—before I realized how bad things were between us. So I tried to talk to her about it later, before she left to go back to the city. She wouldn't then. But a few weeks later I called and invited her to lunch in a way that made it impossible for her to turn me down, and told her I wanted to sort things out with her, and she agreed."*

Sometimes it helps to have a third party present as a mediator—an impartial person, not one directly involved in the outcome. You might ask a counselor, family friend, clergyman, or even a lawyer to serve this purpose—but only after securing your child's permission to do so and agreement on who it should be. But despite your willingness, you may find at first that your child is unwilling to risk the status quo, however intolerable it may seem to you or even to him. In that case all you can do is keep trying—as long as there's life, there's hope.

Compassion and forgiveness—for self and others—require a certain degree of maturity. I sometimes think you have to be a parent yourself before you understand your own parents. It may take our children that long to let go of their resentments and recriminations, their negative feelings about our shared past. Some of the things that trouble them may seem insignificant or even nitpicky to us—and some probably are. Others may have taken on an importance that appears all out of proportion to the hurt they caused. And a few may have faded from our memory so completely that we have no idea what our child is talking about. For years my daughter made reference to a knee injury she sustained at twelve, of which I have no recollection, although she says she was on crutches for a month, something I'm sure I couldn't have forgotten. "It was the day of your first publishing party," she said recently. "I know, because my knee was swollen like a basketball, and you just kept telling me to stop being difficult and pass the hors d'oeuvres." And whenever she feels a twinge in the knee, it's my neglect she remembers, not the injury itself.

REGRET IS GUILT WITHOUT NEUROSES

Remember when they were babies and cried for no apparent reason? They'd been fed and burped and changed and held, but in spite of everything we did, the crying continued. When they were small, we probably overlooked some symptoms of inner distress unless they were manifested in the extreme. And we might have missed a lot that was going on in our family, either because it seemed normal or because we couldn't face it.

That was then, this is now. Now we may notice things about our children we didn't see before, evidence of distress whose roots may lie in the past. We may count some sin of omission or commission as the reason: We didn't love them properly, we pushed them out of the nest too soon, we didn't teach them perseverance or patience or courage or whatever it is they seem to be lacking now.

If we focus mostly on how we might have been partly or wholly to blame for what might have been less than a perfect, problem-free childhood, our guilt will overwhelm their pain. It becomes a story about us, not them. If we can refuse to own the guilt and substitute regret instead, the feelings of shame or self-hatred will recede enough from our immediate consciousness so that we can be available to our children as a source of strength at a time when they need it—a part of the solution, not the problem. As writer

Phyllis Theroux puts it, we're not in the child-rearing business anymore; we're now in the business of child support. When we listen, accept, and acknowledge, we feel regret instead, which is simply guilt without the neurosis.

Making peace with our children involves breaking down barriers so that we can truly hear each other. Much of what we will hear may not be pleasant, especially if they have been harboring feelings of resentment for a long time and this is the first opportunity they've had to air them—or at least the first chance, to their way of thinking, that they've been asked to do so and assured it was safe. The feelings may in fact be exaggerated and intensified simply because they've been let out to air. But we have to let them express themselves fully, not cut them off at the pass because we think we've gotten the gist of what they're saying or already know how they feel. We need to give them enough time to tell us what is really on their mind, which may not be the first or even second incident or issue they bring up. "Treat what they tell you as information, not an attack, and treat their perceptions of you as useful feedback," suggests Gordon. "You don't have to own their assessment of you, but you do have to hear it and, once again, accept that it is true *for them.*"

Most of us, as parents, paid scant respect to our children's views or interpretation of things. Because we were adults and they weren't, we automatically discounted what they had to say, labeling it childish or unsophisticated. But in fact they may have a keen understanding of us, and of the way things were in our families, because they saw and lived the unedited version. A lot depends on how they see the world. One of my kids is very rational, analytical, cognitive, and the other is totally emotion-based. To hear them describe certain things that happened when they were growing up is like *Rashomon*.

Here are some other suggestions from those of us who've been there and back with our grown children:

- Watch for ways in which you and they respond according to roles established early in the family—victim, rescuer, persecutor, peacemaker—and try to avoid those traps.

- Be willing to answer their questions, even if it means breaking silences long held for what seemed to you good reasons at the time or because of what was too painful to face then.

- Guard against the most typical barriers to open communication: defensiveness, denial, counterattack, and unfair comparison.

- Don't triangulate the situation; don't involve other family members, especially siblings, as third parties to the discussion.

- Remember that if you are the one who is committed to changing the relationship, the responsibility is on you, initially at least, to let down your side first. If you don't, they won't either.

COMING TO TERMS WITH OUR OWN PARENTS: THE FIRST STEP

Here's a truth about postparenting: If you haven't come to love, forgive, and accept your own parents, it's very tough for your children to do so with you.

Once when my daughter, Jenny, was suffering the hormonal effects of adolescence, I complained that I'd been thirteen once, and it was awful, and making me go through it again with her was grossly unfair. "When you were my age, did you ever think, boy, when I have a daughter, I'll never treat her like my mom treats me?" she asked. Silenced in the middle of my self-pitying rant, a bunch of those instances flashed through my mind like a deck of cards being shuffled, and I nodded. "Well," said my daughter, "if you're not willing to be thirteen again, you always will."

I wish I could say that that insight turned me into the mother of all mothers, but it didn't. It did, however, bring me up short enough to consider, from the relatively safe distance of early middle age, how much my own upbringing had influenced my parenting behaviors. Some were

43

almost exact repeats of the way my mother was with me; some were misguided attempts at overcorrection by taking extremely opposite stances (which explains why the child of a woman who was obsessive about dust, disorder, and debris lives in a house the Board of Health would condemn if only I let them inside).

Patterns of behavior repeat from generation to generation unless they're actively deterred by intervention. That doesn't necessarily mean professional help, although it may require that. Often enough insight coupled with determination and action is sufficient to break the cycle. So, healing the relationship with our kids begins by healing, or at least coming to terms with, the hurts of our own past with our parents. My mother used to say she'd haunt me into eternity, and I believed her. So I made an effort to finish up my business with her before she died. I didn't want to go on shadow-boxing with the mother I never vanquished, the mother I never felt I could; I didn't want her to take my anger, blame, and unmet expectations with her to the grave. It was difficult for her to hear or accept my story; she was vocal, resistant, proud, and defensive. So I did a lot of necessary struggling with her in my head. As a therapist pointed out, it was the internalized mother of my childhood, not the less powerful mother of my adulthood, that I was dealing with. And once I was able to separate the two—to forgive the one and love the other—our relationship improved.

Some of us never settled our accounts with our parents,

and it seems too late or even impossible to do it now, because they're dead or far away or so set in their ways and their beliefs that we can't change them. But if we're willing to engage sometimes painful memories from the past, it can still be done. It may be a one-sided conversation, but we're talking to the parent in our head, the one who lives in those memories, not as the child we were but as the adult we've become.

Owning and integrating our own past—the good and the bad—is the way we can make the present better. *"Opening up a dialogue with my mother about how she remembers the way things were when she was growing up, and then when I was, was good practice for opening up a similar dialogue with my kids,"* said one woman.

Another, who never got that chance with her mother, recently wrote to both of her adult daughters telling them how it was for her and offering to answer any questions they might have about things that happened when they were children. *"It was instigated by my own realization of how little I knew about what really went on in my family. We were very Southern, and things simply weren't said. I had a baby brother who died that I didn't know about until I was thirty, for instance."* This woman's younger daughter told her there were big blanks in her memory about a couple of years in her childhood. *"With all the emphasis on sexual abuse lately, I immediately jumped to that conclusion and searched my own mind about whether that might have happened without my knowing it. But when she pinpointed the years when she was ten and eleven, I realized that was the period when her father was extremely depressed, and I just wasn't very available to her. He's been on antidepressants since then, but she's never known that, because he wouldn't let me tell them."*

We all remember the past differently, and chances are we will be astonished at some of the ways our children, or even our parents, interpret it. But it's the only way we can begin to understand why and how our children feel the way they do today.

THE WAY IT WAS—AND IS

Sharing our own view of the way it was—the feelings as well as the events—is an important part of the process of reconciliation. Telling our children as best we can what happened in our own families before they were born and during the years of their childhood they might not clearly remember can help them understand us, which is necessary to forgiveness. Admitting that while they were growing up we were afflicted with doubts about our own stability, values, capacities, self-worth, or even that there were crises in the family we tried to shield them from, will help them see us as individuals—not perfect, not awful, just human. This isn't the same as justifying or defending ourselves, it's just sharing. Acknowledgment is a two-way street. Not only can't we change the meaning they've made of the past, but they can't change ours either. Like us they can only listen, acknowledge, and accept; these are ground rules that need to be set and understood as applicable to both parties at the outset. That's how a safe place is created in which to express the regret we feel about the way things were without taking or assigning blame, which is different from responsibility and worlds away from regret.

"What it took for me to reconcile with my son was really understanding on an emotional level that he had been hurt by things I did, even though I hadn't intended that and didn't realize it. I told him how sorry I was that it happened and that I wish I could have kept it from happening. At first I felt like my self-esteem and pride were really at risk, but now I think that in open and honest communication, no one's really is."

Of course we can't really hear our children—or anyone else with whom we're in conflict—if our defenses are up, our justifications and rationalizations at the ready, and our investment in being right stronger than our desire to improve the situation.

WHO'S THE PARENT HERE?

You may be waiting for your grown kids to express an interest in making things better between you. But the longer you wait, the less it's likely that they will initiate it. The distance between you will intensify, emotionally if not physically. The patterns of unsatisfactory relationship will feel even more resistant to change. Your support, understanding, and even love will become less important to them.

They will have learned to get along without it, compensating for its lack in other ways, including some that may be damaging to them in the long run. But who's the parent here, anyway? Standing on false pride is shaky territory, especially when timing is of the essence. And it is. After all, there are a limited number of great years left with your kids, and it would be dumb to miss them.

What's at stake here is the relationship you will have with your children for the rest of your life. It's worth opening a dialogue with them now that can create a good one.

Chances are you will learn something about yourself too. About the leftovers from your upbringing that affected theirs. About what gets in the way of honest communication, not just with them but with your mate, colleagues, friends, and the rest of your family, even your own parents. You may have grown used to, if not happy about, the distance that separates you from your parents if they're still alive, but you want something more real, more honest and rewarding, with your kids.

• • •

To sum up, unresolved hurts from the past may be keeping you and your children from establishing a close relationship today. The longer you let it go on, the harder it will be to heal those hurts and the easier it will be for them to shut you out of their life. So you must take the initiative, with or without professional help. Either way you will need to listen to their version of your shared history, acknowledge it, and accept it as being true for them—whether or not it jibes with your own memory—without justifying, defending, or rationalizing. Sometimes you may need to make several attempts before reconciliation can begin. But this doesn't mean accepting wholesale blame or getting mired in guilt; that allows them to shift responsibility to you, which traps them in dependency and hampers their efforts to stand on their own two feet.

Almost-adulthood offers us a window of opportunity—a period of time not to rewrite history but to make peace with it and get on with growing a strong, flexible bond that can weather the changes in our life and theirs that the future will surely bring.

CHAPTER THREE

WHOSE LIFE IS IT, ANYWAY?

I tossed around restlessly as the autumn wind whistled through the trees outside my bedroom window, surprised by my sleeplessness. I thought of my son and daughter, settled finally in college dormitories on opposite ends of the continent. It had been a long, wearying journey getting them this far, so why couldn't I sleep?

I got up finally and went into their rooms, banishing the silence with a flurry of shaking, dusting, and sweeping, stopping now and then to examine the discards of their childhood—outgrown clothes, old term papers, even, in a corner, a tattered teddy bear. It had always comforted me, that annual autumn rite, as if by changing the linen on their beds and lining their bureau drawers I was making a fresh start for them. But that night the familiar tasks didn't reassure me; in fact they seemed futile. Yes, they would return in time; they would unpack their clothes and hang them in the closets I was rearranging. She would be glad I rescued her favorite sweater from the pile marked for the Goodwill; he would be pleased I replaced the broken glass on his leadership award.

Or would they? I was troubled that night by the idea that there was some essential parental task I had neglected, like taking them to the dentist or teaching them to say "please" and "thank you." But their teeth and their manners are sound, so it could not be that. And it occurred to me that I was refurbishing and repairing a past they had already put behind them—that although they would be returning to this house, to these rooms, they would not be living in them again, merely passing through. And that whatever I forgot to do for them—to teach, show, notice, praise, give, or honor—they must do for themselves, or else do without. And that was why, that night, I could not sleep.

Virginia tells me about Tina, her twenty-year-old, who is spending a year traveling in South America. To date she has contracted dengue fever in Bolivia, had her pocket picked in Bogotá, barely escaped the Shining Path in Peru, fallen in love with several guys Virginia has never met, wired home for money, lost her passport . . . and Virginia is exhausted. "You raise them to be independent, self-reliant, and to think for themselves," she says with a sigh, "and then you spend the rest of your life worrying while they do it."

Well, yes. And no. A certain amount of apprehension is inevitable and even reasonable—the kind that started the first day your child crossed the street alone. But just as most of us eventually stop telling our kids to look both ways, we finally understand that they are beyond our protection. As Judith Viorst puts it in *Necessary Losses,* "Yet although the world is perilous and the lives of children are dangerous to their parents, they still must leave, we still must let them go. Hoping that we have equipped them for their journey. Hoping that they will wear their boots in the snow. Hoping that when they fall down, they can get up again. Hoping." And, as Virginia adds, "All I guess I can do now—all any of us can do for our kids at this age—is be there with a safety net."

HOW STRONG IS THE SAFETY NET?

What constitutes a safety net for an adult child, anyway? "Two parts money and one part love," said Chloe, but who's counting? (Chloe is—when her kids took advances against their allowance, she always charged them interest.) "Knowing he can always come home," said Janet (who hasn't changed a thing in Bobby's room since he left, even though he has a nice townhouse in Short Hills and his father is writing the great American novel on the ironing board in the laundry room). "Whatever they need, if we have it to give," said Pat (who never said no to her kids except once when she didn't hear the question and bought herself a new winter coat before she realized what she'd done and was overcome with guilt). "From each according to his ability to each according to his need," said Sonya, a committed Marxist (whose capitalist sons, successful stockbrokers, bought her a BMW convertible for her fiftieth birthday).

Most parents who can don't hesitate to help out in a crisis, especially if we perceive it as not a direct result of our offspring's actions. But even that judgment is fluid, to say the least: *"Jonathan lost his job as a result of a company merger and had to borrow money from us. Yes, he should have seen it coming and not blown his savings on a Porsche, but it wasn't his fault."*

"Heather left her husband and came home with the baby. She doesn't want to leave him with a sitter, and I have a job, so we've been supporting her. Still, it's not her fault."

"Pete broke his leg skiing. I was shocked to learn he had no medical insurance, so I paid the bills. Of course it wasn't his fault."

Of course it wasn't. Although we have internalized *for ourselves* the values of our parents' generation about prudence, self-reliance, and independence, we judge our children's behavior according to a less stringent credo, nurtured by the Me Decade of the seventies and the "victim culture" of the eighties. For them we want fulfillment, gratification, self-realization. We forgive them not only their sins but also their responsibility. *"I make many more allowances for my kids than my parents would have. They were much more judgmental. When I screwed up, they always said, 'I told you so.' Consequently we had—still have—a very distant relationship. That's not what I want with my children."*

Still, now that the chickens hatched by a generation of permissive, indulgent, process-oriented parents are coming home to roost, many of us, like Carrie, are beginning to run out of patience. *"There are three things my grown kids can count on: a hot meal, a bed for a night, and my ear. Beyond that I'm not making any promises,"* she says. Which has allowed Carrie to love them without weakening their independence, to interact with them as peer rather than parent, to make guilt-free decisions about whether, when, and how much to help them as needs arise.

LIVING WITH THEIR CHOICES

It can be difficult to watch children make choices that seem hasty, unwise, ill considered, or even dangerous. Yet allowing them to do so and live with the consequences is necessary to individuation—ours as well as theirs. A child's individuation is about separating from parental psychic and emotional authority and claiming the autonomous self. Parental individuation is acquiescing in and acknowledging the separation of the adult self from the child's self. This is not the same thing as yielding full control. While physical individuation begins when the umbilical cord is cut, their independence, and ours, is nearly a score of years away.

How we experience separation from our children depends on how old we are, what stage of life we're in, how satisfied we are with our marriage, job, health, even our own parents' situation. In a society that values independence we're not supposed to grieve when children leave. Yet many of us feel as if a death of sorts has occurred. There are no appropriate rituals for mourning the loss of our children or our identity as mothers. The separation is especially painful when the usual rituals of adulthood have been delayed, eliminated, interrupted, or extended. With our children go our hopes for their future, our fears about their ability to make it without us, our concerns about whether we have adequately prepared them for what they will face. And when they leave, they also take with them their own judgments about what kind of parents we have been. As the editors of *Ourselves, Growing Older* write, "Some children leave prematurely, feeling unfinished, by mothers who have overvalued independence. Some leave angry, some by default, others eagerly, supported in their ambitions by the mothers left behind, but accompanied by an internal mother. And by readjusting our fears and expectations, which we must do to live with their decisions, our limits are stretched way beyond what we imagined they were."

"When our kids were young, we controlled them—we had total authority and used it. When they were older, we coached them—we had the power of the pocketbook to reinforce us, and sometimes we interceded in their lives if we had to, just to keep them from making life-endangering mistakes. But essentially they were on their own in day-to-day decision making. Now we have no power at all."

Well . . . not quite. What we have left once they've left is limited influence that derives from the importance, consistency, and duration of our historical relationship; like ex-presidents, we can offer our counsel (if they ask) and our caring (in whatever ways they wish it expressed).

Both counsel and caring are optional. We can't force either on them. Our influence is limited capital. *"I've learned not to spend it on anything less than the big decisions. I try not to butt in, but often they call and ask my advice, and hook me. If I give advice they don't like, they get mad; sometimes they just want me to listen, but I've never been able to do that without giving them advice."*

Most of our children have made choices we disagreed with, ignoring our warnings, threats, fears, and even legal attempts to dissuade them. One woman's son went to Oregon to live in a religious community with a guru and his followers. Another's daughter eloped with a forty-two-year-old biker when she was seventeen. A pacifist activist was furious when her son joined the marines; a strongly religious pro-lifer was horrified when her daughter had an abortion. Here's what they said:

"When none of the threats and warnings work, you don't really have any choice except to accept. Otherwise you lose your kid entirely, and what's worth that?"

"I finally came around to what is essentially a philosophical position, which is that when the only freedom they have is to do what we approve of, they are not free at all."

"You keep experiencing the burden of their choices, psychically if not actually. Sometimes you feel a great deal of pain, but they're doing great."

WHAT'S A PARENT TO DO?

Once our children have reached their majority, they have an adult's right to make their own decisions about how and where to live, whom to love, the kind of work they will do, what to spend their money on, what church they go to, how to raise their children, and even what laws they will follow. Those are not rights we granted them and therefore are not rights we can take away. And the right to make their own decisions carries with it the responsibility of living with the consequences, good or bad. The only decisions for which we bear responsibility are the ones we make.

Successful navigation to adulthood requires the development of functional and attitudinal autonomy from parents; the ability to manage and direct personal affairs with minimal assistance; and the accomplishment of developmental tasks such as completing an education, finding a job, managing personal finances, and establishing separate residences. The self-identification of the grown child is independent from the parent's; emotional independence demands that our children give up excessive desires for our approval. The first adult life structure is formed during the transition between adolescence and early adulthood; according to Daniel Levinson, author of *Seasons of a Man's Life,* it occurs between the ages of twenty-two and twenty-eight. In that period young adults will make choices that will turn out to be dead ends, or wrong, or inappropriate; it is not until the end of the twenties that they will feel the limits of that first life structure and create and take opportunities to change it. Meanwhile, helping a child deal with the fallout from the wrong choice does not give us the right to criticize that choice or try to substitute our own the next time. The following story points out what Judith Viorst explains is the True Dilemma Theory of Parenthood: No matter how much of our life we devote to our children, the result is not entirely within our control.

"My daughter ran away with a no-goodnik when she was sixteen, and her subsequent choices in love and marriage were not much better. She's thirty-two now, she has three children by three different fathers. She is finally putting her life together—working, going to school, and sharing custody of her kids. She is immensely strong, stronger than I thought she was, and although I would not wish her problems on anyone, I can't say she isn't doing really well, maybe because of what she's been through. I've been as supportive as I am able, considering my resources, financial and otherwise. I have helped her with tuition, I take the kids on the one school day she has them, and I took her on a little vacation trip, without the children, right after she got her associate of arts degree. You just have to find the right ways to express that you still care about them—ways they can accept."

LOVE MEANS NEVER SAYING I TOLD YOU SO

Sarah never made a decision her mother didn't make for her until she married a man her mother warned her against and moved across the country with him. Things turned out exactly as her mother predicted, but Sarah, who brought the baby home once, won't come back, because her mother can't help rubbing Sarah's mistake in her face, or bad-mouthing her ex-son-in-law. When Sarah talks about the decisions she has to make now—where to live, what kind

59

of work to do, what to do about day care—her mother undermines her confidence by harping on the bad one she made before and finding the flaws in Sarah's new plans: *"She's just so unrealistic. She goes for the wrong kind of guys—she's seeing one now who makes the first one look like Mr. Wonderful by comparison, and he was pretty terrible. And now she's going to move into a house with two other single women and their children because she can't afford to stay in that house I told her not to buy; it was overpriced, and California real estate has just gone to hell the way anyone could see it would."*

Elliott quit a secure job and started a business with his savings and money borrowed from his friends. At first his parents were miffed that he hadn't ask them for start-up funds, which shouldn't have surprised them because they made no secret of their disapproval. Throughout the brief life of the venture Elliott's mother clipped help-wanted ads that seemed to match his credentials and sent them to him—she thought he ought to get a day job for security and run his new business in his spare time: *"He kept telling me about how Bill Gates dropped out of Harvard and started Microsoft, but my husband, who's been in business all his life, said Elliott was not making smart business decisions about spending so much money on fancy offices, not getting computerized right away, things like that."* Since the venture failed, Elliott has been trying to pick up the pieces of his life and start again, with his father coaching from the sidelines. But his father's experience occurred in a different economic climate, in an earlier time, and in a totally un-related field. And unlike his father, who was a company man, Elliott is an entrepreneur. So parental advice—insis-tence even—on what he should do next is especially aggra-vating, even without the *I told you so*s; it just points out to Elliott that neither of his parents has the vaguest idea of who he is or what he wants.

Few people get everything right the first time, and no matter how mature or competent our children are, they're bound to suffer disappointments and failures. We could not have prevented them, though it probably didn't stop us from trying. We pointed out the pitfalls, the dangers, the consequences, and when they ensued, we told them we saw it coming.

Actually we couldn't have. Because what we predicted was based on remembering our own past—the risks we took and the ones we didn't—and the feelings stirred up by our failures. That's how we learned not to stay out all night and party just before a final exam, not to let ourselves be exploited by people, not to get into debt, and that's how they have to learn too: *"Our experiences taught us things we couldn't learn any other way, and we need to get out of our kids' way so they can learn them too. No matter how many times you tell them, it won't make any difference until they find out for themselves. We want them not to do it the hard way, like we did—but is there really any other way?"*

When we were in school, our math books just had the problems, not the solutions. We had to work the problems out the long way and show the teacher how we got the answer. My children's books had the solutions in them, and even though they were supposed to work the problems out themselves, sometimes they didn't. And they didn't really learn fractions or geometry or whatever. So when we tell our children to take our word for it—don't move in with that guy, he's a jerk; or don't quit college now, it'll be so much harder to go back once you have a job and a family; or don't buy stuff on time, it'll cost you more in the end— it's like encouraging them just to copy the answers.

WHY THEY CAN'T LEARN FROM OUR MISTAKES

We think we are closer to our children in attitude, be- liefs, and lifestyle than our parents were to us. And in some ways we are, simply because we've lived through a cultural and societal adolescence together, rebelling against authority, questioning our institutions, liberating ourselves from outdated notions about what our proper roles should be, and claiming our personal autonomy.

My daughter and I seem contemporaneous in a way my mother and I never were; after all, she was a wife nearly all her life, and all her other roles and pursuits were secondary. Jenny and I are both single; we nourish careers and consciousness with equal devotion. My mother loved and lived with one man; my daughter and I have lived through a wider array of sexual choices. Our politics, values, and lifestyles are remarkably similar, despite the twenty-six years between us. And it has taken me that long to face up to the truth that despite how contemporaneous with her I sometimes feel, she and I are not peers. Economically, socially, sexually, and professionally, Jenny's world—the one she grew up in and the one she lives in today—is as different from mine as mine was from my mother's. My daughter and I are both the New Woman, but she is newer than I am, and that makes all the difference. And when as an adult she makes decisions that will have major life consequences—about career, marriage, children, health— I am galled to discover that it's just as hard to let her make them herself, particularly if I think they're the wrong ones, as it must have been for my mother. The fact is that just as my mother's reality was not mine, neither is Jenny's— even if she and I are both artists and she loves the Grateful Dead too. The generation gap is real; only by standing on our own sides, seeing the distance between us, and ac-knowledging it can we bridge it.

Using our experience as a model for our children is not the same as handing down an article of clothing and ex-pecting it to flatter or even fit them. In fact much of our youthful experience is irrelevant, since it occurred in a very different era, under very different conditions. Our children know more than we did at their age, and respond to situations we faced years ago out of their temperament, worldview, and experience, not ours. So we should not expect them to react the same way. It is in the nature of parents to want our offspring to learn from our mistakes so that they don't repeat them. They don't and they do, and they make others. Whatever they do, they have to work the problem themselves to come up with a solution, and they may have to work it a number of times before they get the right one. Eventually we may even attain the equanimity this woman has: *"Frankly, I give much less of a damn than I used to about the choices they make. Sure, some of them are mistakes, or what seem to me to be mistakes, but in the end most of them are just going to be life experiences, good or bad, and you hope the good outweighs the bad, or the bad gets to be not as awful as you feared. Because you can't really know how things are going to turn out. They all find their own road, even if they have to go up a lot of dead-end alleys first. The best thing you can do for your kids is what you've been doing since they were little: help them predict and understand the consequences of their decisions."*

A woman who advises corporate executives how to empower their employees and stimulate initiative has successfully employed those strategies with her grown kids: *"Instead of talking and telling, listen and question; rather than direct them in how you would do it, coach them to come up with strategies of their own devising. Be brief and*

64

not long-winded, back off if they tell you to or if you're repeating yourself, and avoid after-the-fact criticism."

To which I'd add my own mother's most useful words on the subject: "*It doesn't matter what you tell them, they'll ignore your advice. Don't get mad when they do. Life will teach them the lessons you can't.*"

DEPENDENT NO MORE

Our ties with our children are built on dependence as well as blood and history, and it can be very painful to let go of that dependence. A woman who is struggling to let go of her son admits that "*I look at this big, assertive twenty-year-old, and he's like a stranger. I can only love him by remembering how helpless and vulnerable he used to be. It's a way to recapture that incredible feeling you have when they're babies, of being totally needed by this little being, who is so infatuated with you, who thinks you hang the moon, that you are this great source of wisdom and sustenance.*"

Postparenting requires us to rebind our connection, especially our emotional one, in their minds as well as in our own. We need to liberate them from their dependence, which we can do by refusing to make decisions for them, encouraging them to have close relationships with other people and advisers, and letting them fail. In this way we minimize their guilt at separating from us; they have a right to a separate existence, and we owe it to them to allow them to assert it without feeling that they are harming us. It is a loving act to want our children to lead their own lives.

"My daughter has a close relationship with one of my best friends. She talks over her love life with her, which used to make me very jealous—after all, I'm her mother. But she says my judgment about men is clouded by my own past— two husbands abandoned me, and frankly I don't really trust men—and my friend's is not, which is probably true— she had a good marriage, and has many men as friends besides. It's been good for my daughter to get a different perspective."

Adds another woman, *"I will not tell them something's a great idea if I see pitfalls in it, but I will tell them to ask other people, because I know I can't be objective if there's a chance of failure. And the last thing I always say to them is, 'Ask yourself what the worst thing that could happen would be, and if you can live with that, and if you want it badly enough, go for it.' And if it doesn't work out, I feel for them, but I don't jump in and save the day. I'll tell you, though, sometimes I really have to struggle not to rescue them."*

How do we keep them dependent on us? "By not trusting them to make good decisions, and making them feel guilty about those they make that don't please us, discouraging other adult relationships, setting high expectations of them and withholding love or support if they don't meet them," says Dr. Judith Gordon. "As long as our kids feel responsible to us, they don't have to be responsible to themselves."

BOOMERANG KIDS—ONE STEP FORWARD, TWO STEPS BACK

I couldn't wait to get my first apartment, and neither could any of my friends. So why, we all wonder, won't our kids get out of the house? Or once they do, why won't they stay out?

One reason is that we've accustomed them to a standard of living most of them won't be able to afford for years, if ever. We didn't have such great expectations. Being under our own roofs was what counted, even if the roofs had holes, the furniture was boxes and boards, and the refrigerator didn't contain imported beers and Belgian endive.

There are other factors contributing to the boomerang phenomenon, all of which point out the differences between their generation and ours. They're marrying later than we did, divorcing faster, spending more of their income on nonessentials, staying in school longer, competing for jobs in a retrenching economy, and being priced out of the real estate market.

This "Postponed Generation" has extended its coming of age by at least half a decade, if by that phrase we mean transiting the rituals that spelled adulthood to us and functioning independently. And between young adulthood and functioning independence some of them are coming home to roost, to rest, and—so it sometimes seems—to ruin our lives.

Don't take it personally, if you take it at all. Which is ultimately your choice. Remember Carrie's one night's lodging, one hot meal, and one sympathetic ear? This is a credo Carrie developed after her nineteen-year-old son flunked out of college and came back to live at home. Her litany of complaints is depressingly familiar to other boomerang parents, from the first warm welcome to the last angry "if you don't like it here, you can leave!" She made a deal with Jeff: She'd subsidize his portion of the rent in a shared house with two other people for three months. After that she'd pay half for another three. All his other expenses were his responsibility. And she'd pay his tuition at a community college on the same basis, although he had to buy his own books ("If he pays for them this time, maybe he'll read them," she mused). She got her life back, and Jeff got his own started.

The best thing about boomeranging is that it gives you another chance to foster your child's independence. You do it by responding to the request to come back home again as if you are dealing adult-to-adult, not parent-to-child. You agree from the start on the terms: how long it will be, what expectations you have, and how conflicts will be resolved.

The person who moves back in with you is not the one who left. He has stumbled on the way to adulthood—but he has not failed at it, whatever the circumstances that brought him home. He is disillusioned, disenchanted, and disappointed, which naturally stirs your sympathy.

He wants to be taken care of, and he wants to take care of himself. He may not have broken his attachment to you, although he knows by now he should have. And he feels entitled to whatever you have, which makes you angry when you give it to him or guilty when you don't. In fact he may be genuinely confused that you aren't welcoming him with open arms, refrigerator, and pocketbook—when have you ever denied him before?

If you never have, this may be a rude awakening for him and a hard habit to break for you. Many of us have always given them not only what they need but what they want; it's time now to define the difference, to supply only some, not all, of the former and give the latter sparingly and only on special occasions, even if we can afford it and it places no hardship on us.

Jean Okimoto and Phyllis Stegall, in their excellent book *Boomerang Kids: How to Live with Adult Children Who Return Home,* say that what adult children who return home need from their parents is empathy, a new viewpoint, encouragement to develop confidence and competence, respect for their autonomy, and acceptance of their emotional responses. Here's what we need when they're under our roof: acceptance of the conditions necessary for our comfort, which reinforces the reality that it's our house, not theirs; a way to express our feelings without taking their recrimination or anger; agreement on our personal and territorial boundaries; and an estimated date of departure.

IF AT FIRST THEY DON'T SUCCEED

Because children make some bad choices doesn't mean they can't and haven't made some good ones. It's important for their self-esteem and confidence to remind them of those rather than harp on the ones that didn't work out as well.

People grow in different ways at different ages. Your daughter has her personal life together—she's in a good relationship with a decent guy—but she can't seem to hold a job. Your son knows everything about particle physics and is a rising star in his field, but he can't make a commitment to a woman or balance his checkbook. Your youngest is a psychiatric social worker with a successful practice, but at family celebrations she still picks a fight with her older sister. Your namesake made a bundle in cellular phones and has a great apartment, but he's hardly ever there—he still comes home for dinner, and plenty of nights he sleeps over.

The twenties are the tryout years, and what motivates young people are two contradictory impulses: the urge to create a structure that will serve their needs into the (barely) foreseeable future and the fear of being locked into a life pattern that will ultimately prove unsatisfying or limited. The decisions they make at this point are energized by their strongest inner needs, which differ from one individual to another. Some focus on education or careers, others on their personal relationships, and more than a few these days on finding a spiritual center.

When one young man went to Israel to live in an Orthodox, fundamentalist community, his parents, mildly observant Conservative Jews, were aghast. Said his father, *"From shtetl to Scarsdale to shtetel in three generations— how could he do this to us? What have we done wrong?"*

A twenty-eight-year-old who has tried three different educational tracks and still hasn't finished or focused on one is driving his parents to distraction—and near-bankruptcy. Said his father, *"First it was law school, then med school, and now history. He's the best educated cab driver in Chicago. Just once I'd like to go to a graduation."*

A thirty-two-year-old middle manager who has hit the glass ceiling just informed her parents that she's planning to have a child on her own. Said her mother, *"My husband hit the roof. He said she'd never be welcome here. I simply can't understand why she's giving up so soon. She could still get married and have a baby with someone."*

Our sons and daughters follow their own timetables, and when we don't agree with their priorities or validate that their needs are their own and not ours, we rob them of the chance to shape their own lives. The choices we made that turned out well for us are the choices we want them to make. The ones that didn't work are the ones we want them to avoid. Because that's what we'd do if we had the chance.

We don't, which is the bittersweet part of being a parent. Nor do we have any reliable way to know how the decisions our children make will turn out—whether they will be permanent or temporary, right or wrong for them.

Maybe our spiritual wanderers will find their way home again. Maybe our children's first, youthful marriages will be their only ones. Maybe our can't-decides will find something they can stick with—someone must want a smart nearly-thirty-year-old with two years of med school, a third of a law degree, and all but a thesis in Renaissance history. If our unmarried daughter chooses to have a child, it won't be because it just happened, the way it did for many of us; she'll approach it with more seriousness and forethought. As Judith Viorst says, "Letting our children go and letting our dreams for our children go must be counted among our necessary losses."

HAVE A GREAT LIFE

Many of the problems we have with our children come from confusion about whose problems they are. Getting clear on ownership of both rights and responsibilities can be like untangling a skein of yarn and is complicated in many cases by our willingness to step in and take over problems that don't belong to us. This infantilizes our children to the point where they avoid responsibility for living their lives and presents us with an increasing number of problems we can't and shouldn't solve.

Suggests Dr. Judith Gordon, "Clarify ownership of problems by asking yourself whether you have *present* responsibility for your grown child's behavior; if it infringes on any of your rights or freedoms; and whether your kids have a right to behave as they're doing, regardless of whether or not you approve." If you only answer yes to the third question—which is probably the case, except for children who live under your roof, legal or financial responsibilities to which you are a party, or, sometimes, grandchildren in whom you and your children have a shared interest—then butt out.

• • •

To sum up, our children have an adult's right to make their own choices and have the responsibility of living with the consequences. If we make their problems ours, they avoid that responsibility, and we are faced with problems we can't and shouldn't solve. To be successful adults, they must establish their self-identification apart from us, and we must allow them to give up excessive desires for our approval. While our experience may be useful to them, it is not as relevant as we believe, because they respond to situations we faced out of their own temperament, world-view, and life history. We can help them more by minimizing their guilt at separating from us, by allowing them to fail, by trusting them to make good decisions, and by not harping on those that don't turn out well. We must set rules for our boomerang kids that encourage them to develop competence and confidence. And we must understand that the decisions our children make in early adulthood are motivated by their strongest inner needs at the moment and may not—probably will not—be their final ones.

According to an old Yiddish proverb, "Little children disturb your sleep, big ones your life." You can only let go of your children when there are no conditions attached to your love for them and when you truly accept and understand that their rights and responsibilities are the same as your own. Until that equilibrium is achieved, you will never be more than a parent, and your child will never be more than your child.

Once, that was enough. But if you want a lifelong connection with that person, you must set aside those labels long enough to discover another way of relating to him or her—as a friend.

CHAPTER FOUR

MAKING THEIR WAY IN THE WORLD

The moment they are placed in your arms, you dream the dreams. Their lives unfold before you, covered with glory, riches, and satisfaction. You choose their names with un-confessable forethought—how would this look on a book jacket, in a headline, preceded by an honorific, followed by a string of distinguished degrees? You see him accepting a Nobel, taking an oath of office, saving a life, repairing the world—all in those first few seconds, before he ever opens his eyes. These days, I suppose, you'd conjure similar futures for her, although then, I confess, the years fast-forwarded in my mind; I saw her beautiful in a cloud of white lace and tulle and, later, leading Mike Wallace through the newly refurbished rooms of the White House. As the times changed, so did those images: She would have a room of her own (although what she would do there was never quite clear). She would have a calling, if not a career (but just in case, she'd learn to type).

He had a hat collection when he was a little boy; imagined futures hung from varnished pegs on a wooden tree that stood in a corner of his room—policeman, fireman, astronaut, train conductor, trapper, sailor, Indian chief, magician. She had costumes too—the nurse's whites, the cowgirl's fringed skirt, the ballerina's tutu, the artist's smock. And while they played out their fantasies, I did the same.

The dreams get a grip. You don't let go, not during the years when he wants to be a truck driver, she a cowboy, nor later, when their interests and talents reveal themselves; he can't stand the sight of blood, and she can't be dissuaded from taking your small appliances apart.

Whatever you want, darling, as long as it makes you happy, you say, but you don't really mean it, unless what makes them happy also makes them safe against poverty (can't you write poems or throw pots on weekends, dear?), danger (it's very hard for race-car drivers to get health insurance), obsolescence (logging has a certain charm, but what about the spotted owl?), or political incorrectness (of course someone has to police the streets, but why you?).

We raised them to have big dreams, but often as they take their first tentative steps into the adult world, we are stopping in our own tracks, reassessing the work to which we have devoted twenty or thirty years. "Has it ever been worth doing? Is it still?" These days some of us have hit the wall. We've topped out well below the top of the professional pyramid, we're hitting our heads on the glass ceiling, we're worried about losing our tenuous hold on our own futures, let alone our children's, as corporate America retrenches and all we've worked for, including their expensive educations, seems to have lost its value. We as well as they are wondering about the color of our parachute. In this as in so many other aspects of our lives, we're growing up together. We can't offer them the assurances our parents offered us: that hard work, loyalty, and perseverance will pay off. We can't help them through the career passage since we're stuck in our own. We're caught up in our own mid-life crises, a notion incomprehensible to our parents, who couldn't afford the luxury; it was a measure of their success that they raised and educated kids who could. "Whoever said you're supposed to be happy?" asked a friend's father when his son quit a job that just didn't, well, make him happy any longer. "Why, you did," replied my friend. As he tells it, his father stopped in mid-rant, perplexed. "That was when you were a kid," he said. "Now you're a man. You're not supposed to be happy, just employed."

But of course the generation that greened America expected its kids to be happy *and* employed, although these days many of them are neither. Meaning and purpose, challenge and impact, are important, are what we want for them and what they want for themselves, too, but they're meaningless to a twenty-two-year-old who's pushing hamburgers at McDonald's despite his college degree. This may not be the Great Depression, but it's grim out there, and getting grimmer. In the eighties one of five college graduates was working in a job that didn't require a college education, competing with high school graduates and driving qualifications up; today the figure is one in three. The unemployment rate among college graduates in their early twenties was 4.8 percent in 1990, 6.9 percent in 1991, and 7.7 percent in 1992. Still college enrollments climb, which will increase competition among graduates and gradually whittle down their average pay advantage over those without degrees.

GREAT EXPECTATIONS— WHOSE FAULT, WHOSE FAILURE?

Increasingly our children are finding that their expectations don't jibe with reality, and we aren't much help. After all, by the time we came of age, the hard times our parents lived through were history, and our experience with adversity was strictly secondhand. And even if we hadn't found success that easy to attain ourselves, we felt certain our sons and daughters would. So we praised self-expression and personal fulfillment, valued process over result, were understanding when, instead of facing reality the day after graduation, or even that September, they embarked on their first (and so far longest) career, the search for identity. What we didn't share with them is the one certain lesson life has taught us: that authentic identity derives from facing reality, not ignoring it. "We encouraged them to express themselves and to fulfill themselves," wrote Susan Littwin in *The Postponed Generation,* "believing that somehow sheer abundance would support them. 'They can paint on weekends,' we thought, imagining perhaps that most of their lives would consist of weekends ... We believed in and lived the work ethic, but the message of high expectations was there in the very air [they] breathed. [They] absorbed it osmotically: [They] were special."

That specialness notwithstanding, our children may not manage even to achieve the standard of living we attained through a combination of factors: not just our allegiance to the work ethic but also becoming adults in a boom economy and/or inheriting from our parents. They might not have been millionaires, but the (finally) mortgage-free house that proclaimed their membership in the middle class, bequeathed to us in the dizzy eighties real estate market, represented a much bigger chunk of capital than

79

only the most financially successful among us had yet acquired on our own.

If we made sacrifices for our children, we tried hard not to harp on it the way our parents did. What we gave our kids were high expectations, that sense of specialness, which in turn generated in them a sense of entitlement once reserved only for the offspring of the wealthy and powerful. Neither serves them especially well today and may in fact be hindering them in their struggle toward adulthood.

"My kids have blown-up expectations. They graduate from school and they want seventy-thousand-dollar jobs with hours from nine to three. I haven't put out these expectations, they're culturally induced. My daughter wouldn't blink about buying a two-hundred-fifty-dollar suit for a job interview, and I don't have one that cost nearly that much, but she expects me to give it to her. How as a parent can I give any advice to counter these unrealistic expectations, without stepping on their dreams? Ultimately I think it's their job to figure it out, and my expectations are that they will."

I DON'T CARE WHAT YOU DO, DARLING, AS LONG AS IT MAKES YOU HAPPY, AND OTHER LIES MOTHERS TELL THEIR CHILDREN

My-son-the-doctor and my-daughter-the-lawyer are overworked clichés that speak to parental desires to link their kids' career choices with status, money, power, and social cachet. Yet as much as we laugh at those who do so, few of us resist the temptation to prod or encourage our offspring into vocations that, at least in our youth, seemed most likely to confer or solidify their position in the middle class: *"We worship at the altar of professionalism, undervalue the acquisition of useful skills, deride blue-collar and service occupations as not worthy of our children's talents, and/or project onto them our own unrealized ambitions. My God, we've become our parents!"*

When my daughter took a job repairing Birkenstocks (you'd be surprised how many people will pay five dollars to get one twenty-year-old shoe fixed), I was too embarrassed to tell my mother, who started planning Jenny's career—the first woman chief justice—when she won a high school debate. I told her that number-one granddaughter had found a position in "apparel merchandising." And I'm not the only one. Says a friend whose twenty-four-year-old son is a hospital orderly, *"I tell people he's in the medical field. Are we really such snobs as that? I don't want to be, but after you spend all that money on their education and give them lessons in everything from tennis to French, you want to have something to show for it."*

And this, from a woman academic: *"When I say, 'Whatever you want as long as it makes you happy,' and know damn well I don't mean it—what kind of job is playing a harmonica in a cantina in Mexico for someone with an Ivy*

*League degree in Latin American studies?—I feel just like
my mother. I don't want him to be unhappy—strapped into a
job he hates, like my father was—but there are other things
that could make him happy if he'd try harder."*

WHAT KIND OF JOB IS THAT FOR
A GROWN PERSON?

There are some things we don't want our children to do,
and they're not just the dangerous or illegal things. Michi
the pacifist "couldn't bear it" if her son went into the
military. Marylou the liberal "would die if he became a
fundamentalist minister." But, said the mother of three
children, *"It's all about who your kids really are, what their
abilities and talents are. You get the raw material and then
you nurture it, but it's still just raw material. I have a kid
who's a lawyer and absolutely hates it; this is a girl who
was cutting and pasting and sewing when she was four and
loving it. Now at thirty she's making quilts; she's only a
contract lawyer when she needs money. That being I gave
birth to, the one with the interest and skill in sewing, is who
she is, not the lawyer she tried being to please me. I see how
much happier she is making quilts, and I'm glad she's doing
it. The world has plenty of lawyers who are miserable."*
The way many of us feel about the choices our children
make about jobs and careers often reflects the persistence
of values instilled in us by our own parents, who didn't

expect work to meet their deeper needs or express their inner desires, just to pay the bills and put something away for the proverbial rainy day. Those traditional values conflict with our expanded vision of what work or career should be—an experience of personal growth, an expression of the essential self: *"It's like there are two voices in my head when I think about my kids, who are both looking for work now. One is my parents', which says, 'Get a job with a company that pays good benefits and has a retirement plan,' and the other is mine, which says, 'Do what you love, the money will follow.'"*

Her husband amplified her comments: *"I know, I say it too. But I don't think we're all as sanguine about this as we say we are. We know we don't want to put pressure on them to get jobs that will make them miserable, but haven't we put too much of a premium on only doing something that will make them happy? I mean, they don't call it 'work' because it's easy!"*

THEY JUST DON'T UNDERSTAND HIM

In sorting out their own priorities, our sons and daughters are often reacting to the mixed messages we've given them, not only about their careers but also about their capacities. It's a rare parent who can see his or her child clearly and objectively. At a school board meeting I attended a few years ago, the only definition of a gifted child on which everyone in the audience could agree was "mine!" Based on that subjective judgment and on our own closely held beliefs about the kind of work that is most likely to yield our children the kind of life we want them to have, we often attempt to chart their future and persuade them that our choices are theirs. When the fit is a good one—when what they want and can do jibes with their abilities and our desires—conflict is minimal, and success is, if not assured, at least possible. When it is not—when they are unsuited by temperament, interest, or talent to the life plan we've drawn for them—their attempts to find their way to a right livelihood will continue to elude them. We must curb our tendency to bring our own values to their search for meaningful work, because when we insist that those are the only valid ones, we make it harder for them to identify their own values: *My son was so locked into my dreams for him that it was long before he dared dream his own, and it took me a long time to hear what he really wanted and to encourage him to go for it.*

"The most important thing you can do, as a parent, is to step away and try to see who your kid really is, not who you want him to be," advises Ellen Wallach, career counselor. "Because by the time he's in his twenties, his abilities are probably pretty clear to those in a position to hire or encourage him. You can open doors, if you're able, but you can't push him through them. And if he doesn't fit once he's inside, all you've done is set him up for a blow to his self-esteem."

Rarely do our children turn out to be the way we dream they're going to be. Which is exactly the point. If we really want them to be happy, we have to trust them to be the best judges of what makes them that way, consistent with the realities of having to support themselves and meet their responsibilities. Continuing to rescue them from these responsibilities—like the woman who has been paying all her son's bills, including his child support, while he tries to be a rock-and-roll star—may make them happy but won't make them adults. And, suggests Susan Littwin, "You may resent the fact that your children are still dependent and confused at an age when you had real adult responsibilities. That doesn't mean you have to enable them to go on that way. You can stop taking care of their unpaid bills or finding new jobs for them when they get bored. But you can also stop thinking about what they ought to be doing and criticizing them and giving them unwanted advice. You can't nag them into adulthood. The very nature of becoming an adult is such that no one can do it for you."

MY HAIRDRESSER'S COUSIN KNOWS THE PERSON WHO'S HIRING

Opening doors is tricky, yet what parent wouldn't give a child a boost up if he could? Not the women I interviewed. *"I absolutely wouldn't hesitate to pull any strings I could. My husband and I get around a lot, we hear things—this company is looking for someone, or that one is. I helped my older daughter get a job in the theater by contacting some- one I read in the alumni magazine from my college was a producer, and if I knew someone in publishing, I'd call them to help my younger one, who's been looking for a job for months. Say, do you . . . ?"*

We can be utterly shameless about buttonholing people we think could be helpful to our kids: *"In this world it's who you know as much as what you know. It's not as if my kids wouldn't be good at whatever they did. I'd be doing whoever hired them a favor."*

"I wouldn't try to help unless my daughter asked me to, because I think she should exhaust other channels besides influence first. But if she wanted me to, yes, I would. I have a lot of women friends with very good jobs who have con- tacts, and I would ask them. When she wanted recommen- dations to college, I called in a few favors, but I wouldn't have done that unless I was sure she'd live up to them."

Those of us who aren't in a position to open doors for our kids would, too, if we could. But since we can't, we look on the bright side: *"I wish I had the connections or influence to help them. I'm jealous of people who do, but I'm a realist— that's the way the world works. I just tell them, it's like having to work your way through college; it makes you appreciate what you've accomplished even more, because you did it yourself."*

We all agree that before we cash in any chits on behalf of

our children, we ought to ask them. But in practice we sometimes don't. *"My husband talked about our son to a friend who had a job available in his company, and when he'd set up an interview, he told Neal, who was furious. It took a long time for that relationship to heal itself."*

A lawyer who is extremely active in her community will ask anyone once on behalf of her children, but only once: *"If they screw up, that's it. I make it really clear; this is my reputation, my friendships, my chits. One of my kids said, 'That's too much of a burden. I'd rather not have your help.' He said it without anger, and I took it that way too. But I have another who blew it; he took a job I helped him get and then didn't show up or showed up late, I'm not sure. But he was fired, and he's never asked me again."*

Most of the women agreed that their husbands, if they had them, were much more skillful at using personal connections or asking friends and acquaintances outright for help for their kids entering the job market: *"I think I'm more likely to worry about how bad I'd feel if our kids screwed up, or that it would reflect on us if they did, than my husband is. Also, it's his field, he knows more people than I do."*

THE PERPETUAL GRADUATE STUDENT

Most parents who can afford it will help their children acquire the skills or education they need to get a job or improve their present circumstances.

"I have a twenty-eight-year-old who left home after high school, got married, and returned after a divorce five years later. She came back to go to college, and we were happy to provide support, although we insisted that she work part-time and pay her own rent, which we wouldn't have done if she'd gone right to college at eighteen. She did well and got her degree and has a job now. It doesn't matter what order it happens in; the culture puts a trip on us about linear progression, but the expectations of society today seem to be that they can be older when they do things we did earlier."

She is much more sanguine about paying college bills for a fully grown child than this woman, whose son has switched graduate schools so often she can't remember the last one: *"He was going to be a lawyer, and then a doctor, and then a teacher. I can't count the money we've spent on his education. See, that's a value I inherited from my parents—whatever else you do or don't do for them, make sure they have a good education. But when is it enough? My husband says, 'I wouldn't mind going to school myself. It looks like a pretty easy life.' And every time we say, 'No, we're not going to support this.' But every time we do. He has every right to have a career crisis, but how much longer do we have to pay for it?"*

Not that long, certainly. Prolonged schooling has given many of our children opportunities to extend their adolescence long after it might reasonably be expected to have ended. While government and private sources for funding higher education have decreased significantly in the last ten years, there are other options besides parental gifts or loans: *"There is money out there, if they look for it. My daughter got her graduate degree through a program of matching funds established by her company. My son joined the military in order to get qualified as a pilot."*

"I noticed that when I was paying the bills, my kids didn't treat school as a job. They didn't do that well; they were motivated only by the desire not to be out there in the work force."

"My thirty-two-year-old daughter is in law school now, and we're helping, but we insisted she pay for the first year herself and get good grades before we chipped in. And we consider the money we're giving her a loan; we have a repayment schedule worked out that goes into effect as soon as she passes the bar exam and gets a job."

THE TRYING TWENTIES:
MAKING THE FIRST CHOICE

When my son, Cameron, was very young, he sometimes accompanied his great-uncle, an old-fashioned country doctor, on house calls. Probably what he most enjoyed about those excursions was the fuss that was made over him, the chance to be with a beloved relative, and the stop for ice cream on the way home. Yet from that I imagined for

him a career in medicine that nothing, including his repeated failures at chemistry and math, dispelled. I treated
every passing career fantasy he shared with me as superficial and irrelevant, so intent was I on my own. What he was
doing—what most adolescents do—was trying out images
of himself as a self-sufficient adult. I wasn't hearing or
seeing him as anything more than a projection of my
idealized ambitions—not for the unique individual he was
and is but for the son whose success in a prestigious career
would reflect mine in raising him.

"Career-choice issues become so emotionally heated
because they're a way for parents and children to let go of
each other, and for the children to develop and grow independently," says Dr. Sandra Eller, a psychologist and professor of psychiatry at the University of Rochester Medical
Center. When we overreact to even their transient or superficial career choices, they get extremely defensive about
them. And no matter how logical our arguments, adolescents and young adults see them as an affront to their
independence and respond accordingly.

*"My twenty-four-year-old daughter was tossing out all
these scenarios recently: She might get a job in a boutique,
she might go to graduate school, she was thinking about the
export-import business, she really wanted to design fabrics,
and so on. I tried to discuss each one of those scenarios,
suggest how to structure her résumé and her job search,
whom she might talk to—all this advice she really didn't*

want, because she was just talking to hear herself think. Finally she said, 'When I decide what it's going to be, I want to know everything you know that could help me, Mom, but I have to make that first decision myself.' She just wanted a sounding board, not a career counselor."

My own daughter finished college, managed a year of travel in Asia, and had a hard time finding a job when she returned. After a few months she applied for a position teaching English in Japan, reasoning that it would support her desire to keep traveling and could be picked up or dropped at will. "But you're just postponing real life," I protested. "Has it ever occurred to you that this *is* my real life?" Jenny answered.

As a matter of fact it hadn't, since I was seeing her "real life" in terms of being "settled"—in a city, a career, a relationship. Said the mother of her best friend, a woman I've known for years, *"We impose on our kids what we think are the benchmarks of being grown up, but what it comes down to is, that's so we don't have to worry about them."*

Actuarially speaking, nineties college graduates will have at least nine different careers before they leave the work force, many in jobs and fields that haven't even been invented yet. They have noted the wholesale firings and downsizings of the post-eighties world and give short shrift to the idea of corporate or career loyalty. Many of them are carving out careers, or at least paying the bills, in ways and means we don't often take seriously, often because we never had a chance not to take our careers seriously.

"When I was in my twenties, it was the fantasy about opening a restaurant, or running a bookstore, or going back to the land and raising sheep you'd sell for wool. I went to college, and to law school after the kids were born, and while it's not a fabulously rewarding career, it's a living. Now, my son, who had a job with a software company, was laid off, but instead of looking for another job he bought an espresso cart—where we live there's one on every corner, a bunch of kids standing out in the rain peddling coffee. He's a married man with a child—what kind of job is that for a grown man, an engineer? I mean, he didn't even look in his field. But he thinks it's great, so who am I to step on his dreams? One of these days he'll grow up and get a real job."

He may not. Plenty of jobs we don't think of as real, or suitable, appeal to a generation of kids who've seen the empty promises at the end of the corporate or professional road. "Unlike an earlier generation, their self-esteem isn't tied to a work identity," says Marilyn Kennedy, a career consultant. "They are not galvanized by issues of unfairness or social injustice that sixties people would confront an employer on. The ones that have marketable skills ignore that stuff. If the company or the job has values they find repugnant, they take their skills elsewhere rather than confront. They don't define themselves by what they do or who they do it for, the way many of us do."

In the twenties our young-adult children form their first adult life structure, which is rarely the last one; if they are either not happy or not successful in their careers and relationships, most of them will make the necessary changes. Roger Gould describes this period as one in which "most of the simple rules of life often prove ineffectual— life's supposed-to-be's are not realized." Yet, he says, this is also a time when "new personal development directions are experienced." And isn't that, after all, what we want for them?

The dichotomy between the values of our parents and those forged during our own adult years have put us in a quandary when it comes to our children and their careers: *"We know that having a job you'd do even if they didn't pay you for it is the best of all possible worlds. We also know that much of the world's work is devoid of meaning and purpose, yet we know someone has to do that work. We do plenty of it ourselves. We just don't want our kids to have to."*

We have resolved this dichotomy by imposing a new standard on our children: What you do isn't as important as how you feel about it. Do what you must, but do it whole-heartedly. "I tell them Buddha's definition of right liveli-hood," said Peggy. "Work that is consciously chosen and done with full awareness and care." Michi quotes Anthony

Trollope: "It's important for a young person entering life to decide whether he shall make hats or shoes, but that is not half as important as the decision whether to make good or bad hats or shoes." Or, in Emily's words, "You can change the reality by changing the way you perceive it. You can add meaning to the most meaningless task."

That may be Pollyanna-like thinking, but as another woman said, *"In an economy like this one, where can you look except on the bright side? Unless they're lucky enough to have a true talent or vocation and are able to make it pay, these kids have to make the best of what's out there. And if the best isn't that great, they have to find a way to live with it, or find something better."*

• • •

To sum up, we differ from our parents' generation in our attitude toward work. We believe it should be meaningful, fulfilling, and afford self-realization. Yet we also know that in a contracting economy our children may have to take what they can find, the way their grandparents did. Our daughters and sons have high expectations, for which we feel at least partly responsible. At a practical level there is little we can do except help them clarify their career goals, use whatever connections we may have to help them get started, and realize that the first choices they make may not, probably will not, be their final ones. And emotionally we have resolved the dichotomy between two conflicting sets of values—ours and our parents'—by promulgating a new standard of success: What they do isn't as important as how they feel about it.

We educate them, we try to empower them psychologically, we listen to what they want to do and advise them to do it. More than that we cannot do. The economics of the next century are still unclear. How can we give advice on something we know very little about? We say to them, "What are your expectations? What do you want in life, and how are you going to get there from here?" It's their job to figure it out, not ours.

CHAPTER FIVE

BY LOVE POSSESSED

When my son was still a baby and my mother was patting lotion into the soft, sweet folds of his skin, fastening his clean diaper and tickling his tummy with a noisy smooch, she looked up at me over her grandson and smiled through the tears in her eyes. "Somewhere in the world, right this minute, there's a girl baby with a spit curl right in the middle of her forehead and chubby little legs, whose mother is changing her diaper too," she told me. "And someday that girl baby is going to grow up and take this little darling away from you."

Nothing makes grown women as sappy as a first grand-child, so I laughed off my mother's dire prediction. Until that same little darling brought a young woman home to meet me. She was wearing a DKNY suit instead of a diaper, and her hair was blunt-cut to her shoulders, not spit-curled. Her legs might have been chubby a long time ago, but now they went all the way to the floor. I recognized her immediately—it was that same girl baby my mother warned me about all those years ago.

My suspicions were confirmed when, after what passes these days for a decent interval—the second day of a three-day weekend—they announced that they were going to be married.

"I don't know what to say," I murmured.

"You might start with how happy you are for me—for us," he prompted. And so of course I did. I mouthed all the right words—well, some of them, anyway—and if by the end of the evening I hadn't fully redeemed myself, at least I hadn't said anything stupid. *(What do you mean, married, you're still a baby! Who is this girl and what do you really know about her? You have your whole life ahead of you, you might meet someone else. At least two European princesses are single, if a bit long in the tooth. And there's my friend Hannah's daughter, whom you've never met, an M.D. plus a Ph.D., and she speaks three languages.)*

I don't know why I was so surprised. He'd had girl-friends before, though he'd never lived with one. *(Thank*

God, they're moving in together first. Some hair in the sink, a few spats about money, his moodiness, her PMS— anything could happen.)

I thought of the girls he loved before this one—the small, blond, pretty things who looked at him adoringly, agreed with everything he said, wanted only to please him. Yes Dears, I called them *(though never to their face of course, or his).*

And I always supposed he would take a wife early, knowing his need to create the kind of family he never had and always longed for. *(But didn't we settle that long ago? Didn't I go to Indian Guides father-son banquets. Didn't I find you a Big Brother. Didn't I bring you whole out of a broken home? Didn't I?)*

But not this early. How often I still look at him and see the boy he was, but not the man he has become. He's little less than half my age—how could he possibly be adult enough to take a wife? He has not finished school or chosen a career. He is still in the process of becoming. *(As are we all of course, but still . . . how can you get married when I still have to remind you about your annual dental checkup? And when you still call home collect?)*

There are some men who need to be married in order to begin their lives, and probably he is one. At least he'll never grow into one of those bachelor Peter Pans who at mid-life are still frightened of commitment. *(I know I've complained about them for years. But they're way older than you are—what's your hurry, anyway?)*

It's very clear; he wants to be married now. He yearns for the security of conjugal life, a safe harbor in a stormy and unpredictable age, a nourishing and sustaining love that will strengthen him for the task of claiming his place in the world and confirm his identity as a mature, responsible, functioning adult. Everybody wants that—even I, who am still wondering what I'm going to be when I grow up. *(Finally I have the answer: a mother-in-law.)*

And it will happen, with or without my blessing. Which this lovely girl so charmingly beseeches, thanking me for him—this man who so clearly loves and respects women, who believes they are his equal. It's unusual, she says, it must be my doing.

(Well, of course it is, how else does a man learn that sort of thing except from his mother?)

"She is a feminist like you," he tells me proudly. *(Yes, but can she type? It's perfectly all right not to make the coffee, unless she expects to stand on her principles while you support her.)*

"She doesn't want to be just a housewife. She's very ambitious," he adds. *(What's so terrible about being a housewife? It was good enough for my mother, wasn't it? Before all that business about who made the coffee, it wasn't such a bad life.)*

They want a partnership, they tell me. *(Does that mean you'll be cooking your own meals and ironing her silk blouses too? How do you ever expect to get anywhere in your career with a partner instead of a wife?)*

I don't know what that is, a "partnership." Not firsthand at least. My own marriage was made in a different time, with different hopes and expectations, and when the rules were changed in the middle of the game, it came apart. So I'm no expert. Nor a cynic either—I believe in romance, and even in marriage. *(And it doesn't matter if I don't know what a partnership is, as long as they do, and he takes out the garbage.)*

I always thought he'd choose a Yes Dear. Not only for the comfort, but because she'd be the opposite of me. *(I wasn't Mrs. Portnoy, understand, but not June Cleaver either. I guess this means it didn't hurt him all that much.)*

But not this girl; she'll challenge him. Push him. Even— I wonder if he knows it—nag him. She could be me, except that I was never that composed, collected, sure—not then at least, and hardly ever now. *(Except she's chewing on her lower lip the way I do when I am nervous. And she's squeezing his hand so tight, her knuckles are white.)*

She repairs to the ladies' room to reapply lipstick to her chewed-up lower lip. And ponder, most likely, on whether I like her. I remember myself at her age, meeting my husband's mother, wondering the same thing. *(She had her doubts, as it turned out, but we made friends in time.)*

He isn't worried. Or if he is, it doesn't show. He hopes I'll welcome her into our family—even, by dessert, come to love her just as he does.

It's true I've never seen him this happy. *(Not since the Christmas he got the puppy.)* This proud. *(Not since he won that leadership award in high school.)* This loving. *(When was the last time he hugged me that wasn't at an airport?)*

I wonder if he'd like to give her his grandmother's ring, what I will wear to the wedding, and what their first child will call me.

(If she breaks his heart, I'll kill her.)

NOBODY WILL EVER LOVE YOU
THE WAY I DO

Nothing changes our relationship to our grown children as significantly as the decisions they make about love, sex, and marriage. Creating a new family is a child's ultimate statement of independence, the definitive claim to a life of one's own. Few of their life choices will set off stronger reactions in us, and fewer—perhaps none—are as beyond our influence, let alone our control. While they may seek our approval, it is not essential to their happiness; if we withhold our acceptance, it will make much less difference to them than it will to us: *"Certainly it won't stop them. I did everything short of threatening to disown her, but when it came right down to it, the only choice I had was whether or not to go to the wedding. She's never done anything before that was so against our will. It just goes to show you, hormones are stronger than we are."*

Said a successful woman who has always enjoyed a very close relationship with her daughter, *"She didn't bring the love of her life home to meet me until she was sure of her decision. She wanted to solidify the relationship first, because she's acutely aware of how much my approval matters. She wanted to be really bonded first, and she was. She made it clear: 'This is not discussable. This isn't going to be like it was with all the other guys before him. So what do you think of him?' "*

If being capable of loving and making a commitment to the one you love is a benchmark of maturity, why aren't we happier when our kids do it—especially if, as is statistically likely, they are probably older, at least chronologically, than we were when we married? While we may have accepted their sexuality, welcomed the succession of boyfriends and girlfriends they've brought home over the years, and hoped, even prayed, they'd marry and live happily ever after, the announcement that they've settled on a life partner—even if no ceremony is immediately contemplated—often makes us uneasy in a way all the preparation leading up to this moment never did. *"It's not that I wasn't happy for her, or didn't adore him—I was and I did. But I had a deep sadness, which surprised me—it was like grief. People would say, 'Aren't you happy?' and I'd answer, 'Oh, yes,' but underneath that was a sense of 'I'm lying.' "*

In the best of all possible worlds we're delighted with the news that our child has found true love. The object of his or her affections is worthy and appropriate, the timing is right, the circumstance optimal, and our biggest problem is what to wear to the wedding. It isn't until we've vacuumed the last speck of rice from the living-room rug that it strikes us that the particular configuration of people we call family has undergone a drastic revision. Our position as the most important person in our child's life has been preempted; we are no longer next of kin. The primary bond our grown child has made, legal or putative, replaces the primary one he has with us, and while many other factors may color our feelings about this connection, that's the one that drives the others. And the more we hear things like "You're not losing a son, you're gaining a daughter," or "Aren't you glad she's finally off your hands?" the more our feeling of being pushed aside grows.

"My mother always told me, 'No one will ever love you the way I do,' and maybe it was a self-fulfilling prophecy, because nobody ever did. It's absolutely true, though—no husband, nor any wife, either, ever has as unselfish a feeling or is so willing to throw themselves in front of a speeding car for you as your mother. It's this total, bedrock devotion

that you feel for your child that nobody else can ever feel. I think where we go wrong sometimes is holding out that standard to our children, that that is the way a spouse should love them, and anything less is undesirable. It just sets them up for dissatisfaction when the other person turns out to be less sacrificial than we were."

Marrying off a child—or redrawing the dimensions of family to include a significant other, whether or not a ceremony legalizes the union—not only changes our relationship to that child, it alters our view of ourself, setting off one of those existential crises that calls into question who we are, what our role is, what the reason for our existence may be. No matter how much we've fantasized this moment, how full in other respects our lives may be, we feel abandoned. Redundant. On a downhill slide. Sometimes we project these emotions onto our kids or their new mates; more often it's our own husbands or lovers who get the fallout. We reexamine our own love relationships and sometimes find them wanting; without the kids to talk to, through, or about, we may find there is little else to say. Along with the pleasure we take in our children's happiness is more than a modicum of jealousy, which we try to deny because we don't think we should be feeling it.

"I think when my daughter got married, I was a little envious. She has a wonderful, really honest relationship with her husband, they are partners in a way we never

were. Also, she had a fair amount of sexual experience and a number of other relationships before she settled down, which I never had, and I guess my jealousy about that surfaced. After the wedding was a very hard period for me in my own marriage; it also coincided with meno- pause, so I guess I was really emotional. I separated from my husband for a few months, and in that time I even had cosmetic surgery. I felt terribly alienated from my daugh- ter. I couldn't share her happiness without feeling this awful jealousy. When I was separated, I went out with a lot of men, and I made sure she knew about it. I guess I was being very competitive, although I wouldn't have ad- mitted that to anyone. Finally I guess I came to my senses, I reconciled with my husband, who was going through a similar thing, although it was much harder for him to admit it."

For most of us the joy of seeing our children embarking on lives of their own with the mates of their choice is strong enough to erase our grief at what we perceive as our loss and our envy of the freshness of their love. The contrast between their even imperfect love and our own is heightened, but, say the authors of *Our Families, Our- selves,* "The way couples develop after kids leave is an outgrowth of how they have lived their marriage all along. [The marriage of grown kids] may bring relief or conflict, or make the distance between a couple clear;

couples without diversions or buffers who've spoken through their kids now need to speak directly to each other." Some couples, they add, begin to treat each other like kids; others become middle-of-life adventurers, acting inappropriately youthful, fighting the aging process unrealistically. For single parents, marrying off a child may bring greater opportunity for loneliness as well as for adventure. But for many couples the marriage of their children is an event that renews and revitalizes their own marriages: *"While I am happy for them, I'm even happier for myself. I feel like I've fallen in love with my husband all over again, and he with me. We've weathered the worst of it, we feel a lot of pride that we have, and we've been on a second honeymoon since our youngest child left on his first one."*

WHAT DOES HE SEE IN HER, ANYWAY?

"My first thought when I met the girl my son married was, 'Why did he choose her?' I guess I formed my first impression based on how different she was from me—did this mean there was something about me he hated? And then when my daughter got engaged, I couldn't help comparing her fiancé to my husband and noticing how much like each other they were. As it turns out, I was wrong on both counts!"

Since we are in the habit of taking responsibility for our

children, we assume that they make the choices they do in response to the experience of love or marriage they've gleaned secondhand from us. While chemistry has a great deal to do with the object of their affections, so, too, do their inner needs, "which we can't meet now, even if we knew what they were, and probably couldn't meet then either," says Dr. Barbara Mackoff, a psychologist.

"I'm not sure I interject myself in regard to my daughters' choices in men, but I certainly do in relation to my son's. He's gone out of his way to avoid any woman like me or his sisters, but who he chose turned out to be the image of my mother, the Princess Queen. She's always on the couch, wrapped in a quilt, but she manipulates him the way my mother manipulated my father and all of us. With her he's like we all were with my mother— 'Can I get you anything? Can I possibly make you happy? Can I do enough, give you enough?' In fact she's running the whole fucking show, which I point out more than I should, how much he's like me, wanting too much, caring too much."

Or as someone else said, *"We see our sons' choices as being in reaction to us— 'Oh, good, he finally found me,' or 'Oh, gee, he's too much like me!' "*

We are somewhat less inclined to view our daughters' choices as indicative of their relationship with their fathers: *"I think girls pick men less on the basis of what their fathers were like than sons do wives. My son-in-law is very different from my husband—culturally, intellec-*

tually, in their tastes and interests as well as how they treat their wives—but my daughter loves them both, and admires them for different reasons."

We also think our daughters seek in their mates whatever they perceived as lacking in our marriages, especially equal attention to the needs of both partners: *"My daughter flat-out told me she would not put up with having her needs ignored in her marriage, and she doesn't. I have learned a lot from watching her interact with her husband, and I've tried to instigate some changes in my own relationship with mine based on that. It has not been easy—after all, I've kept silent for a long time—but even the slow progress is worthwhile. My husband and son-in-law aren't that different, it's just that she trained him earlier than I did."*

Said the twice-divorced mother of a recent bride, *"She's fabulous with her husband, she does what she wants. I wish I could do that with my relationships, make them be what I want them to be. She doesn't take a lot of stuff from him the way I always took it. And she has much better boundaries in her marriage. I never felt a man could love me without my being his secretary, therapist, maid, cook, and lover, but my daughter does things or doesn't do things I'm afraid men leave their wives for. But at least she's not phony with him the way I was."*

NOT OUR KIND OF PEOPLE

While many women expressed dissatisfaction with their children's choice of partners, few of us feel that differences in class, race, or religion matter as much to us as they did to our parents. *"I would have been disowned for marrying out of my religion. My sister did that, and my parents sat shiva for her—they mourned her as if she had died, and my father never talked to her again until my mother's funeral. He refused to come to my son's wedding because he married a Gentile. I think it's very sad for him, and while I wasn't thrilled with the marriage for other reasons, that certainly wasn't a big deal for me. But then I'm not as religious as my father is."*

"When my daughter moved in with and then got engaged to a black man, I felt that it was a bad idea, but not because he was black. It was because he was much older than she, had three children by a previous marriage, and she was only twenty-one and had never lived on her own. She accused me of being racist, and I said, 'Oh, no, you can't get away with that. We have always had very close connections with black friends. We've encouraged diversity in your friendships. We lived in Africa for several years when you kids were young. And you simply will not trot out that crap on us.' "

"It isn't an issue to me that her husband is Hispanic.

There's liveliness and vigor there that's brought a lot into all our lives. What disturbs me is the macho attitude he has, which attracted her at first but has gotten to be a problem. It's a real cultural difference. His brothers hit their wives, for instance, and although I don't think he ever has, I worry about it."

We pride ourselves on being tolerant of a child's marriage out of family class, color, and creed; we are less so when we believe the values of our kids' mates are extremely different from our own: "*It bothers me more that he never reads a book, that he's completely estranged from his own family, and that he's something of a gambler, while we are very close-knit, value the life of the mind, and are extremely prudent with money.*"

"*She is extremely money-hungry. She made a big fuss about a diamond, and he went into debt for it; she constantly nags him to buy things they can't afford, and frankly she appraises my things like she's measuring me for a shroud.*"

"*She's just not our kind of person. But still, as long as she makes him happy . . .*"

AS LONG AS THEY'RE HAPPY

Despite our opinions—and sometimes because of them—our children have to live with the partners they choose. And the bottom line for all of us is that as long as those partners give our kids what, after the dust settles, we want for them—a loving companion in good times and bad—we can live with their choices. We must, if we want to keep them in our lives: *"I did everything I could to change her mind, but once she married him, I shut up. Couples have enough trouble putting their marriage on solid ground without in-laws undermining it."*

And we do: *"I just keep my mouth shut. As far as I'm concerned, when you're married, you owe your allegiance to your spouse, and I don't interfere. She has done some good things for him; she's pushed him into them, but they've been positive. I see her changing a little bit, and that helps too. And no one, except maybe my daughter, could tell from the way I treat my daughter-in-law that I don't think she was made in heaven for my son."*

Our society's norms strongly endorse the belief that the solidarity of the marital pair should take precedence over either partner's family of origin; with the strong norm of noninterference in the life of a nuclear household, parents usually become relatively uninvolved in the daily life of their married children, according to sociologist Colleen Johnson. "The intimate marital dyad remains quite private from parents, and couples deal with their parents jointly rather than independently." Which is a good thing if you can't stand the way your son-in-law sits on his behind watching football while your daughter does the dirty work, or your daughter's lover is slightly to the right of Attila the Hun and you're a charter member of the ACLU.

WHY PEOPLE TELL JOKES ABOUT
MOTHERS-IN-LAW

"My daughter's marriage didn't change things between us. We have remained close, and it's actually been easier relating to her as a married woman, more like peers, even though she lives two thousand miles away now. We took a trip together, and we talk on the phone once or twice a week. But I feel very distant from my married son, even though he lives in the same city. My daughter says I'm jealous of his wife, and maybe that's true, although I hate to be such a cliché. I just feel irrelevant to his life, whereas I feel a part of hers. It's just the opposite for my husband, who has grown closer to our son since his marriage and more distant from our daughter, because he isn't a big fan of our son-in-law."

This not atypical experience bears out the findings of sociologist Vira Kivert, who says that for both men and women, relationships with mothers-in-law appear to be the principal points of stress in most American marriages. In a family with son(s) and daughter(s), a son's marriage tends to strengthen the mother-daughter bond by focusing a mother's hostility on her daughter-in-law. Her data is supported by Nils Nydegger in a later study: "Although the father/son-in-law relationship is the model source of tension among middle-class families, the most serious intrusions to the family unit are caused by wives (daughters-in-law) alienating their husbands from their families." In other words, "The queen is dead. Long live the queen."

But happily many mothers report a very different experience: *"Because of my daughter-in-law I see much more of my son than I used to. He's more attentive and available, and I credit her for that. There has been a quantum jump in family closeness since he got married. Fortunately he married someone who is very connected to her own family, which is a big one, and they've just added us to that group. We feel we have gained not just a daughter but an entire clan of wonderful people. We went to Christmas dinner at their house last year, and I looked around and thought, 'This is right out of Norman Rockwell. It's the big, happy family I always wanted when I was a kid, and now I have it.' "*

When my own son got married, our relationship was transformed; rather than distancing him from me, it drew us closer, as it often does with single mothers and their sons. "Having a love of their own makes it safer for them to love us," says a therapist who was single for most of her son's life. "It breaks the cycle of emotional dependence on mothers that can provoke anxiety in grown sons."

In-law relationships are strained when we aren't able to reorient our loyalties and recognize that we owe allegiance not just to our child but to the new family he or she has begun; when we see the new spouse as an interloper who stands between us and our grown kid; when we force our kids to choose between their partners and their parents: *"It's a battle we can never win, and we shouldn't want to, because if we win, they lose."*

DIVORCE WARS

It's very hard to watch children suffer the breakup of their marriages or primary relationships, regardless of how we felt about their partners to begin with: *"If you loved your son or daughter-in-law, you hurt for both of them. My sympathies and my loyalties were really divided when they split up. It made my son angry when I expressed that to him, but it's the way I felt. He'd brought this terrific woman into my life, and now he was taking her away. He said, 'You're still my mother—whose side are you on, anyway?' And to tell the truth, I was on hers, although of course I couldn't say that. I just kept hoping they'd get back together, and when they didn't, and he remarried, I found it very hard to accept his second wife."*

If children's marriages bring about a transfer of their loyalties to their spouses, their divorces transfer them back to us, a gift about which we are of two minds. *"My son was so dependent on me after his divorce, it was like he was a child again. He came back home to live, which lasted about four months before I said, 'You're a grown man. You knew how to live on your own before you got married. It's time to do it again.' I had to push him back out of the nest, and it was hard, but absolutely necessary."*

"When my daughter left her husband, she became Daddy's girl again. Of course we wanted to help her, but after a while we realized what she needed was to help herself. She wasn't as mature as we thought—something we didn't realize when she was married, because marriage hides a lot from public view. I was seeing some aspects of her that I hadn't seen before, and I didn't like them all."

A child's divorce engenders a redefinition of other relationships besides the one with his or her ex-spouse. In-laws, kin, and grandchildren are realigned in new configurations, often to our sorrow: *"I became much closer to my ex-daughter-in-law, at first as a way of staying connected to my grandchildren and then because I really admired the way she put her life back together. We still see each other—I even went to her second wedding. I feel somewhat disloyal to my son, though, and I haven't resolved that to my satisfaction."*

According to Colleen Johnson, marital changes in households initiate changes in the relationship between parents and their grown children. Divorce decreases the level of privacy in nuclear households, so the actions of our kids are more observable to us and others. Divorce and remarriage entails processes of societal reorganization; estrangement occurs in some relationships, and new solidarities develop in others. "These changes in turn shape and redefine relations between parents and adult children, and these events illuminate dimensions of parent-child relationships that are not as apparent in more stable times."

We help our children heal their broken hearts by listening, refraining from taking sides or making judgments, and encouraging them to form other relationships that foster intimacy and connection: *"It's a real temptation to try to replace what they've lost by overmothering them. At first they'll lap it up, but if it goes on too long, it's not healthy for either us or them. It's like when they were kids and fell off their bikes—you make sure there are no broken bones, and then you urge them to get back on. I think we tend to infantilize our kids when their love relationships go sour, when the best thing we can do for them is help them take responsibility for what happened and restart their adult lives."*

All of our children will love again, and most will remarry, engendering even more complicated kinship systems of which we are a part and more changes in our relationships with our children. Once again we will be less paramount in their lives, which will be filled with an increasing number of new relatives; the levels of distance and intimacy between us and our kids change as their marital status changes. *"It was kind of bittersweet after the divorce; my daughter and I got very close. She needed me, and that was wonderful, but I hope she doesn't ever need me in that same way again if it means she has to be that unhappy too."*

THE RIGHT SIDE TO BE ON

When our children have trouble in their relationships, the best thing we can do is keep our distance. Because after the dust settles, if the marriage or partnership lasts, they are going to be sorry they breached the privacy of their union by bringing us into it, and we are going to be sorry too: *"When my kids were having marital problems, they wanted me to take sides, but I wouldn't. I remember telling my mother something I shouldn't have—that my husband had had an affair—and it colored her feelings toward him so that she could never like him again. Long after I'd forgiven him, she hadn't."*

Commented another woman, *"Maybe because I'm a therapist, my kids unburden their marital secrets on me. I have told them I'd be glad to refer them to someone if they want counseling; I'm their mother, not their shrink, and I can't be helpful to them in either context with those kinds of difficulties. One night my daughter-in-law called and asked if she could spend the night—it was clear they'd had a big fight. When she got here, I said, 'I've drawn you a hot bath and made up the guest room, and here's a Valium, but I don't want to know the details, because in the morning you'll be sorry you told me.' "*

WHAT IF THEY'RE GAY?

Recently I spent an evening with two women friends and their mothers. One of those friends has a son who is gay, and when she told us about his new lover, her mother blanched noticeably. It wasn't news to the older woman— she has known of her grandson's homosexuality as long as her daughter has. "It was the way we talked so openly about it that disturbed her," Ellen said later. "She said, 'But you make it seem so natural.' "

Well, it is and it isn't. Certainly both the sexual revolution and the personal-psychology movement have transformed the way many of us think about homosexuality and made it easier for us to deal with gay children than it might have been for our parents. But still, asked the mother of a gay daughter, *"How do we know that? Yes, you put the best public face on it you can. You tell yourself that what matters is that they're happy, you try to be supportive so they can feel positive about themselves, you even tell yourself that they're in a good relationship. But I defy you to find me anyone, man or woman, who would choose homosexuality for their child."*

I couldn't, and probably you can't either. But that's the

point: It's not our choice to make, if in fact it is a choice, which the best evidence suggests that it isn't. An individual's sexuality is part of his or her deep, core sense of self; it is not a parent's to control, and at this stage of a grown child's life (if ever), not his or hers to influence.

With resiliency we believe our parents would not have shown, we are generally positive and supportive of our children's homosexuality—at least the mothers of gay sons are. With our daughters we are more equivocal, perhaps because many of us appear to believe that lesbianism is more volitional and circumstantial than male homosexuality: *"Maybe we just cling to that. Certainly my daughter has been confirmed in her lesbian identity for a long time, since she was a teenager. I don't see anything changing it, although it would be nice if it did."*

"I always thought my daughter turned to women because she could not find a good relationship with a man. I also hoped it was a stage that would pass. Still, I tried to be supportive; I welcomed her partner into my home, and we both liked her. Recently my daughter has started seeing a man, and frankly I don't know what to say to her. If I confess my relief, she'll accuse me of having been a hypocrite all along, pretending to go along with her choice. But I don't know this man yet. I may not like him at all, and wouldn't that be a kick in the pants?"

Ultimately what the parents of gays want for them is what we all want for all our children—a loving, mutual, life-enhancing partnership. And most of us manage to control our qualms about the particular perils of their lives, from discrimination to disease.

"I remember seeing a Gay Pride march when my son was fourteen, and in a difficult phase, and thinking to myself, 'How'd you like to have to deal with that?' Because I guess I knew someday I'd have to. I wasn't really surprised when he came out. But until he found a partner, I was terrified . . . AIDS. Now that he has settled down and is in a monogamous relationship, I realize that it wasn't his being gay I had so much trouble with, only the idea that he would never find someone to love and value him. A lot of the relationships in the gay community are pretty superficial, it seems to me. I truly love his partner too—more in fact than I care for my daughter's husband. The grandchild thing entered into it, especially for my husband—you know how men can be about carrying on their name. But that isn't as important as the fact that he—my son—has a good relationship, is healthy and happy."

JUST WEAR BEIGE
AND KEEP YOUR MOUTH SHUT

To sum up, our children make their choices of romantic and sexual partners based on their inner needs, which we can neither know nor influence. We are less concerned that their partners share our racial or religious backgrounds than we are that their values match ours and our children's. And while they may seek our approval, it is not essential to their happiness; if we withhold it, we will only distance them from us.

When they marry, the bond they make with their partners replaces their primary bond with us. Our own marriages come in for reexamination and may be significantly altered; certainly our relationships with our children are. We can be most supportive of their marriages and liaisons by reorienting our loyalties and recognizing our allegiance, not just to our children but to the new families they have started; by not perceiving their spouses as interlopers; by not attempting to force our children to choose between their parents and their partners; and by allowing them to maintain the privacy of their marriage.

When they divorce, they may become dependent again. Although we may feel temporary pleasure at this new intimacy and at our being once more the source of wisdom and comfort, we hope they will do better next time. Rather than dwell on their failures or allow them to sink into dependency, our task is to help them take responsibility for what happened and restart their adult lives.

When a grown child loves and/or marries, we step off center stage and into the audience. We no longer have a starring role in their lives, which is both a relief and a source of anguish. We may love their partner or not, it doesn't matter—we don't have to live with them, they do.

Kids have a hard enough time as it is without our interfering. If we want to keep them in our lives, we have to accept their choice and do everything we can to support them. I think the best advice I got on the subject came from my son when I asked him how to be a good parent to him and his soon-to-be wife: "Just wear beige and keep your mouth shut."

CHAPTER SIX

YOUR MONEY OR YOUR LIFE

I was on a beach in Bali the Christmas after my mother died when I heard her wry, amused chuckle. "Hey, big shot," she said, "you're having a good time on my money, aren't you?" Startled, I looked skyward; I didn't really expect to see her up there, but her presence was strong, and there seemed to be a trace of her favorite perfume in the air. And when I grinned and answered, "Uh-huh. You'd have loved this," my kids looked up, too, and said, "Thanks, Gram."

Like most people whose financial position improves as

the result of a parent's death, I felt a vague, free-floating guilt about my inheritance; not an uncommon reaction, according to psychiatrist Ned Hallowell, author of *What Are You Worth?* But I had no qualms about spending "their" money on this trip, which I otherwise could not have afforded. I'd traveled frequently with my parents when they were alive, and those journeys were more than the sum of their miles—they were the times we were closest and happiest togther. In faraway places we were able to step out of our accustomed roles and enjoy each other as friends, even equals, in ways we couldn't on their home ground or mine. We were our best selves then. I felt most appreciated, most seen and loved by them on those occasions, the way I want my children someday to remember me.

Or at least that's the way I justified it. It is hard to use money I still think of as theirs in ways they might not have approved, but spending it on my children creates no such conflicts for me, because it didn't for my parents. Travel, like education, was part of what Marcia Millman, a sociologist and author of *Warm Hearts & Cold Cash: The Intimate Dynamics of Families and Money*, calls the "cultural capital" that parents who worked their way into the middle class in the fifties transferred to their children. With that capital we also inherited their values about money; while we may have modified or even rejected those values, they still deeply influence ours. For example, although many of our parents willingly sacrificed their own material comforts or even their security to ensure our own, we are less likely to do so. And while we understood their warnings about saving for a rainy day—after all, they suffered through the greatest depression in history—until recently such caution seemed irrelevant to us. It is the rest of their legacy—seven to eight trillion dollars that has been or will be transferred to us and our younger siblings in the next twenty years—that is forcing us to reexamine what we owe our grown children. We are rethinking how we feel about our future and theirs; whether we have indulged them too long; and if we should continue to do so. Sandy's story is a good illustration of how we are struggling with these issues.

Sandy's parents were hardly rich. They lived on their pensions and Social Security until they died four years ago. Still, her half of their estate—savings bonds they purchased once a month starting the year she was born and a house they bought for seven thousand dollars in 1947—leaves her more than comfortable enough to help her children, a twenty-five-year-old son whose wife is expecting a child, and a twenty-six-year-old daughter who is unemployed. "Because I can, I guess I should," she says. Yet she worries that giving her daughter money is a mistake: "As long as I support her, she'll never have to support herself." Her son and his wife would like to buy a house, but they don't have enough for the down payment: "If I give them the money, how will my daughter feel?" She is remarried to a man whose son is in college: "Do I have an obligation to help educate him? After all, Frank didn't help pay my kids' college tuitions."

Similar questions plague other families who have profited not from parental inheritances but from their own hard work and good fortune in entering the labor force during the longest period of economic expansion in this century. A couple who still live in the house they bought when the first of their five kids, now ages twenty-two through thirty, was born, are eager to sell it. They have plans for all the equity they've built up, but three of their children are living at home, one who never left, and two who came back: *"How much do we owe them? We put them through college, we gave them a good start in life, and someday they've got to be independent. I just hope that day comes while I'm still around to see it. Meanwhile I keep dreaming of all the things we could be doing, we should be doing, with the money that's in this barn."*

Regardless of how well off we are, whether we earned our place in the middle class on our own or secured it with even a modest legacy from our parents, most of us worry more about our children's economic security than our own. We've already bought our houses, raised our families, and have or are making provisions for our retirement. Barring unforeseen catastrophe, we think we'll be okay, but we aren't sure they will be. We've been telling them all along to do what makes them happy, because we assumed that the economy would continue to prosper and expand. But now that the rainy day our parents warned us against has finally arrived, we wonder if we were wrong: *"My daughter, who's twenty-five, is an artist. She lives from hand to mouth, and she's always managed to survive, somehow. I couldn't handle such financial insecurity, but it's the cost of the life she's chosen, one that makes her very happy and fulfilled. Still, I worry—what if she gets sick? She has no health insurance. I sent her to art school because that was what she wanted; and frankly I thought she'd marry her boyfriend, who was in medical school. I mean, I know it's important for women to be able to support themselves, too, but there is enough of my mother in me that underneath I probably think it's not as important as it would be for a man and that for women a career is of secondary importance to a husband and family. Now I think I was wrong. I should have pushed her to study something more lucrative, like computers. When I told her I'd be glad to do that now—underwrite more practical education—she put her finger on what I was thinking: She said, 'Oh, since I've broken up with Bill, you think I'm going to be an old maid, right?'"*

DOING THE RIGHT THING

These stories illuminate our concerns about how the way we employ money with our grown kids affects our relationship with them and their ability to function in the world without us. We know from our own experience that money can either knit generations together or tear them apart. We believe that the way our parents allocated or transferred their wealth to us—or didn't—expressed the way they really felt about us and, in some instances, their effort to control our lives even after death.

"By making my brother the trustee of my inheritance, my father made it clear that he didn't think I could be trusted to make my own decisions, although I was forty-seven when he died."

"My sister was always the good girl, and I was the bad one. She got not only all the money, but the house too. The only thing he left me was a small insurance policy for my son's college."

"When my father left everything to my brother and sister's children and nothing to mine, it was obvious that despite his liberal bullshit, he really disapproved of my marrying a black man."

Most of our parents weren't wealthy in their lifetimes (their paid-up houses were their major assets), but all of them made sacrifices for us—or at least they told us they did, and we grew up believing it. We have been more ambivalent about that. While we may have deferred gratification to some extent in order to provide our children with what we thought comprised a good life, it is more likely that we purchased the extras by taking jobs outside the home. The emotional rewards of joining the work force—

the empowerment and increased self-esteem we felt—far outweighed our sense of sacrifice. In a strong economy, with at least one breadwinner and often two in our households, we rarely had to choose between our children's material comforts and our own. And while we understand this has imbued many of them with a sense of entitlement, as we and they get older, we don't feel a strong need to maintain them in the style to which we accustomed them.

"Maybe I'm selfish, but I don't feel any obligation to provide my kids with the same standard of living it took me years to achieve, especially if it means a big sacrifice on my part. My son could have gone to an Ivy League college if I'd been willing to use up my savings or go into debt. I decided I wasn't going to, although I did pay his tuition at a state university. My mother thought that was terrible of me; I said to her, 'Look, if he wants to go badly enough, he'll work or take out loans.' In eighteen years I never owned a new car or took a vacation or spent much money on myself. But frankly it's my turn now. My parents went without a lot in order to give me everything, and they really guilt-tripped me—I felt like I was an investment that had to pay off. I had to get the best grades, marry the most successful guy, be the most beautiful and accomplished. It was a lot of pressure. I wouldn't do that to my kid. Or maybe that's just a rationalization."

We are not ungrateful for what our parents did for us when they were alive or for what they may have left us when they died, but we are keenly aware of how they used money to express not only love and concern but also guilt, control, anger, disappointment, and, yes, sexism—and we are determined not to repeat it with our children.

Again the double bind of our generation—the clash between our parents' values and our own, heavily influenced by the empowerment movements of the seventies—has shaped our expectations, assumptions, feelings, and behaviors about money, just as it has about many aspects of our parental role. We know that money is powerful and that, properly used, it can enhance rather than hinder the close, caring connection we want to have with our kids and can foster their maturity and independence. We want to use whatever resources we have more wisely than we think our parents did. We want to be fair, to treat our children equally, even when their circumstances are not equal, even when our feelings about them are not equal. We want to do the right thing—right for us and right for them. The difficulty, as we shall see, is knowing what the right thing is.

SECURING OUR FUTURE

How much is enough to secure our own future is a question we can never quite answer, because we can't know how long we're going to live. So how much of that we can spare to help our children, or just make their lives more pleasant, depends on the assumptions we've made about the future and the degree of comfort we feel about our own financial condition. We worry most about the prospect of being dependent on our children, an acute concern for those of us presently coping with the infirmities and dependencies of our own aging parents: *"I'd like to help my kids buy a house, but not if it means I can't stay in my own for as long as I'm able to. My grandmother lived with us, and it was a big strain on everyone. But she'd made my father promise he'd never put her in a home, and he couldn't afford it anyway, so he didn't. I will not burden my kids that way. So when my kids ask for money, I tell them, 'If I give it to you now, you'll be sorry later.' But if they really needed it, I'd go into my old-age fund."*

Of course we all define "need"—ours as well as theirs—differently. Because we've spent most of our adult lives in an expanding economy, we're less worried about our financial future than we are about theirs. While Social Security may be bankrupt when they need it, we believe it's solvent enough to see us through: *"If we were more optimistic about the future of the economy, we'd be spending our money on ourselves, now that we've fulfilled our responsibilities to our kids. But our kids won't even live as well as we did. If it's a choice between an apartment in Florida or college for my grandchildren, I know what I'd choose—their college. But my husband says we're moving to Florida, and that that's our kids' problem, not ours."*

In fact her husband echoes the feelings of many of our

spouses, who want a break: *"I broke my balls getting them raised. With their education and all the advantages they had, they ought to be able to manage for themselves. It's my wife who thinks we shouldn't spend our money, we should leave it for them."*

They are much less worried than we are about how well our kids will live: *"It will be a challenge for them, no doubt about it. I did what I thought would equip them for that challenge, and they're smart kids. They'll figure out how to get their children educated. If I've got it, sure, I'll help. But they can't count on it, and I want them to know it."*

Right now, we're still earning money, and our old age is a comfortable distance away. We may be able to help, even support our children if we have to—but should we?

Generally we base those decisions on our pocketbook, our patience, the pleasure it gives us to give them what we want them to have or to support them in something that will make them happy and fulfilled—a house, a graduate degree, a business opportunity, an extended period before they have to deal with real life—and whether or not we feel we have a real choice about it.

A CHOICE, NOT A DUTY

"If it's a choice between my kids living on the street or my paying his rent, of course I'm going to pay his rent."

Shelly's twenty-six-year-old son, Colin, is one of those

marginal not-quite-adults called "slackers"—a social dropout, a bright rebel who barely gets by, someone whose main activity is hanging out, who just doesn't want to grow up. That's how Colin's father, Charlie, describes him. Shelly's take on her son is quite different: She thinks Colin is emotionally disturbed. He is her sensitive, vulnerable first-born, whose depressions have disturbed her since he was an adolescent. They've urged psychiatric assistance on him steadily since then, but except for one brief period he's refused it. They are both teachers with limited incomes and no significant assets except their house. Although Shelly says money's never mattered to them, both she and Charlie are nervous about whether their savings will be enough to see them through their old age. Because Charlie worries more about that than she does, Shelly acquiesced in the ultimatum they've given Colin—six more months, and he's on his own. "If he's really too depressed to function, he'll have to see a doctor to get SSI assistance," says Charlie. "That's what I paid taxes all these years for. And if he's just lazy, he'll have to get off his ass."

And if he doesn't? "You can't just close the door and say, 'You're on your own,'" says Shelly. "I think we would continue some kind of help, especially if he gets treatment. And we'd pay his health insurance—we've done that for all our kids until they had jobs that provided it. If they didn't have insurance, I couldn't

133

sleep at night. But if your kid really can't make it, it's not a choice, it's a duty. It doesn't stop just because he's grown up."

KEEPING THEM TIED BY THE PURSE STRINGS

Some children can't let go of their parents, and some parents can't let go of their children. When they are grown up, money becomes the medium and the metaphor for continuing the state of dependence. Said the father of a twenty-six-year-old who made many attempts at establishing her own independence but was restrained from doing so by his inability to let go, *"I supported my daughter until I cottoned to the fact that I was afraid that if she didn't need me anymore, she wouldn't have any reason to stay connected to me. I told her I would only pay for college if she went to the state university, a few miles away, instead of the school she wanted, at the other end of the country. Later I wouldn't let her live in the only apartment she could afford. I told her it wasn't safe and talked her into a more expensive place she could only manage with my help."* At his wife's insistence the family went into counseling together, and the daughter was able to articulate her fear that if she left, her father would die, and his that if he let her, he'd lose her.

In some families money is the way parents and children act out separation issues that were not resolved at the end of a child's adolescence. There are children who can never detach from their parents, which sometimes reflects the problems they are having in other areas of their lives, such as school, work, and relationships. And there are parents, particularly those who have been divorced, whose adult children are their main source of emotional support. These parents often encourage financial dependence because they fear abandonment: *"Sometimes when you're writing a check (to your grown child), you have to ask yourself, 'Who am I doing this for?' And if it's for you, not them, you shouldn't be writing it."*

As we grow older, we modify our internalized values about money in ways that underscore the differences between the generations: *"My parents made decisions about giving us money based on whether they approved of what we were doing with our lives. I am really aware of that as I make similar decisions with my children. I don't want to lay my trips on them—that I think they should live one way or another, that they should have something or not. Still, I can't get entirely away from that mind-set—I'm only human, after all! When one of my kids wanted to take an expensive advanced computer training, I loaned him the money, but I didn't charge interest. When another one wanted to buy a sports car, I cosigned a loan at the bank. Another time my daughter said she needed some money but didn't want to tell me why. I respected that, but we went to the bank and she took out a loan against a CD of mine. In all three cases they paid back the loans. It is a weird way to do things, but we're all pretty comfortable with it; it's a way to deactivate my control-the-kids button."*

WHEN I SAY NO, I FEEL GUILTY—MAYBE

Our attitudes about giving our children money can be compromised by the degree of guilt we feel about ourselves as parents, by the attention, affection, and stability we've provided them, by the difficulties they faced growing up, and by ur own concerns about having treated them fairly or eqι ιy. Distributive justice—how limited resources are distri¹ ed fairly among disparate claimants—is a major deteι inant of how we allocate our money to our children. In wʰ ʾat Dr. Millman calls the "intimate dynamics of fami-lies nd money," the justices of need, equality, and reward play shifting roles. And so, too, do our unarticulated guilts and regrets.

"I give more to my daughter because she never got as much as the others. I was going through a divorce, my life was a mess, and I always felt I neglected her. I have a lot of guilt about that, and even though I know I can't expiate it with money, I do it anyway."

"I am overly generous with her because she doesn't have as good a life as her sister—she doesn't earn much money, she isn't married, she hasn't many friends. I don't think my

gifts make up for what she's missing, but if they give her a little pleasure, that's better than none."

Aware as we are of trying not to use our money to control our children's lives, we have a hard time when we're asked to bankroll plans or purchases we don't approve of. If we say no, we feel guilty—unless the money is for something so outrageous, ill advised, or against our deepest principles that we have plenty of justification for our denial. And even then, we may say yes, but will attach conditions that assure us that our children are assuming risk, too, or otherwise make us feel more comfortable about it. We make it a loan rather than a gift, charge the equivalent of bank interest, and hope our misgivings don't turn out to come true.

According to Dr. Judy Barber, a family therapist who specializes in the psychology of money, "Parents should ask themselves why they're making a loan instead of sending their children to a bank and giving them a chance to find out about the real world. If you're using your money as a means of keeping strings attached or if you sense that your child is afraid to make the emotional break, perhaps a loan is not in either of your best interests."

Even when it is, it may be wiser to introduce your children to your banker than just to write a check. Using your CDs or stock certificates to help them secure loans in their own name, or cosigning notes for big-ticket items such as houses, cars, or business investments helps them build their own credit and allows you to maintain your own assets. Keeping complete documentation, following IRS guidelines when establishing interest rates on loans between family members, and evaluating both the reason for the loan and your child's ability to repay it, are important. But most important is being realistic about whether or not you can afford to live without the money: *"It's so hard to say no. I've gone without on several occasions so I could give my kids money, and even though I didn't think I minded, the truth is that I did. And that resentment hurt our relationship."*

THE LAST FRONTIER OF SELF-DISCLOSURE

Banks don't have to explain every detail of their finances to a prospective borrower, nor do you, if you don't want to. But children often have no real idea about their parents' financial situation. As my daughter said, "I always thought you got richer when you got older—automatically, like vintage wine." If we had money worries when they were growing up, we kept them to ourselves as much as we could; we didn't want them to worry too. And if we have them now, we don't tell them, either, if we can avoid it. So they may believe that we are much better off than we actually are. They can ask with impunity, and if we turn them down, they think it can't be because we can't afford it but because we're trying to control them or make judgments about them.

If we've been especially closemouthed about money, they may also be worrying about whether, at some time in the future, they'll have to provide for us. Being more open with them about our general financial health makes sense; it may cut down on unnecessary requests for loans or handouts and relieve them of their unvoiced but very real concerns about being fiscally responsible for us in our old age. It is also a way to let them know that we think they're adult enough to be taken into our confidence: *"I had to take over my mother's financial affairs when she got sick. I was stunned to realize how close to the bone she'd been living. It made me very sad to realize that I could have made her life much easier, and would have, if I'd only known. It's really important to level with your kids before that day arrives."*

We set our own standards for how and why we give or loan money to our children; this is the issue on which we have the most divergent strategies:

"I try to evaluate requests like a banker would. If I think a banker would turn it down, I either say no or I give it as a gift, with no strings attached."

"I have a thousand-dollar limit on loans from my own pocketbook. The terms are the same—one year, at five percent, and no more than two loans in any year. I don't want to know what it's for or why they can't find the money

somewhere else. If they need more than that and can explain what it's for and how and when they'll pay it back, I'll go to the bank with them. But frankly at this stage of my life I'm ready to withdraw from active lending. I'd like to feather my own nest, not bankroll my kids."

ALL IN THE FAMILY

The book value of a family business is more than dollars and cents. What doesn't show up on the balance sheet is the satisfaction of knowing that something you've built will outlive you; that you've provided your children with a way to earn their living; that you've established a context for keeping the family together in the future. And despite the clichés that are legion—the siblings duking it out in the boardroom, the tyrannical father refusing to yield control, the children who have turned their backs on the business but demand an equal share of the profits, the incapable or incompetent son or daughter—the family business that works does so because it possesses an inborn competitive edge no other company can match. Writing in *INC.*, Leslie Brokaw reports, "A business run by a team of family members is more resilient and more likely to succeed than any other kind of company. . . . Despite the emotionally taxing challenges of family-based management, there are things about how family businesses function internally and are perceived externally that other businesses simply can't replicate."

Brokaw cites several reasons for the inherent strength of family businesses: the individuals understand viscerally what makes their compatriots tick, which breeds speedier management; the "star power" family members have with customers; the continuity and stability they demonstrate that make employees as well as customers feel secure; the sacrifice and resilience during a long-term crisis that is typically demonstrated by family members, who are in it for the long haul; and the inherent trust that produces a stronger team.

Still, family businesses can also be fraught with emotional and financial peril for everyone involved; only one out of three family businesses survive from the first generation to the second, and only one of those will make it successfully into the next generation. Certainly the state of the economy has much to do with a company's survivability, but so do more subtle factors:

"I don't think my son ever really wanted to go into the business, but he just couldn't bring himself to be up front about it. Consequently he ran it into the ground. If he and my husband had ever been able to tell each other the truth, we could have saved a lot of grief, as well as a small fortune. They weren't even talking to each other when my husband died."

"My kids' personalities and philosophies just didn't fit the family business. But we almost went bankrupt until we figured that out."

"The children thought of the family business as this perpetual money machine, and they expected to come in and take over the controls. But they had no vision beyond being rich."

"My husband couldn't ever stop seeing the kids as kids. He couldn't give them responsibility or accept their suggestions or criticism, particularly when it had to do with aspects of his own personality he couldn't accept. They never got credit for good ideas, and they got blamed when things went wrong, even when it wasn't their fault."

The most successful family businesses turn to outside planners and consultants, not only for help with strategic corporate planning but also for guidance in planning for transition and succession, which can be emotional mine fields. Carol and Tom, who are the second-generation owners of a thriving nursery business, started that process when their children were in college. They were all offered jobs—"starting jobs and starting wages—I wasn't having any twenty-year-old with a company Gold Card," said Tom. Two of his children joined the company, with clear plans to take over the management eventually. The one who did not was invited to participate in family councils with the understanding that her eventual inheritance would consist of stock her brothers could, if they chose, purchase from her at fair market value when their parents died. "I wanted them to know I was going to treat them fairly, but 'fair' isn't the same as 'equal,' " Tom said. "If she didn't want to assume any responsibility, I didn't think she should continue to be a voting shareholder."

In another family, whose children expressed no interest in continuing the business, plans were drawn up to sell it when the parents retired. Company employees would have the first right to purchase, and some stock would be distributed to longtime employees. The proceeds from the sale of the business, like the parents' other assets, would be divided equally among the children at their death.

"You can never create a plan in the middle of transition," says Thomas Hubler, president of Hubler Family Business Consultants. "It actually creates family disharmony not to have a plan, and eventually it almost inevitably leads to an explosion and recriminations within a family. When my firm is brought in, it is generally because of problems that have bubbled up in the business, but the solution is more often in the family relationship."

The rewards of a family business are more than just financial. Working together on behalf of a common goal binds generations together, keeps lines of communication open, and provides a shared context for mutual support and affection. But there is also a downside risk to consider, as Carol says: "If a business falls apart, it's a pity. If a family does, it's a tragedy. What you need is a plan and a process that takes into account which is more important and how each will survive even if the other doesn't. That is, if we're fighting about family issues, we can't let it impact on the company—and in the case of a death or divorce, we've got to have a coping strategy. Conversely if there are problems in the business, you can't let that set one family member against another."

WILL THEY ALWAYS CALL HOME COLLECT?

To sum up, despite the recent downturn in the economy, those of us whose high earning years occurred during better times are more worried about our children's economic security than our own. And many of our generation have also inherited the nest eggs our parents saved for a rainy day. If we are therefore in a position to help our children financially, we are also keenly aware of the feelings that money expresses. We know that how we use money with our children has emotional as well as financial ramifications in our families. We want to do the right thing about money, but we aren't entirely sure what that is, and we are ambivalent about the idea of sacrificing our present or future comfort to keep our grown children in the style to which we have accustomed them. Our husbands, especially, are less inclined to continue indulging them than we are.

When there are unresolved dependency issues—ours as

well as theirs—money often becomes the medium and the metaphor. Money is often the way we act out separation issues. And while we do not want to do what many of our parents did—use money to control our children's lives—we still base our decisions about loans or gifts on whether we approve the uses to which they put it. We often express our feelings by the terms of the loan—whether we charge interest, steer them to a bank, cosign loans, or set limits above which an explanation is required.

Distributive justice is a key determinant of how we allocate our resources among our children; that is, our sense of choice is often influenced by guilt about how we've raised them, by how much we love them, and by how vulnerable we feel they are.

Many of us are not forthcoming with our children about our true financial situation, which often leads to misunderstandings. Sharing some of this information with them is useful, both in cutting down their requests for money and in relieving them of worry about whether we will someday be a financial burden to them. And while it may not be necessary now to make a full disclosure, as we age, it will be.

Family businesses often illuminate the many diverse strategies we have for dealing with our children about money. And despite the taxing emotional challenges of family-based management, the businesses of this type that work do so because of an innate competitive edge. The most successful ones typically employ outside consultants who specialize in family enterprises to help manage the transition from one generation to the next and avoid the intrafamily squabbles that divide and conquer family strength and connectedness.

• • •

How do you know when your kids can make it on their own? When they do. When they come to you as a last, not a first, resort. When they stop asking you for a loan to cover the phone bill, the rent, or an overdrawn check. When they buy you a present and it's not your birthday or Christmas. When you spend your own money on yourself without worrying that they might need it. When they leave your house without the contents of your freezer or your extra toothpaste and shampoo. When they ask you if you need money. When they buy their own health insurance. And when they finally stop calling home collect.

CHAPTER SEVEN

WHY CAN'T THEY BE FRIENDS?

In the cemetery where my parents are buried, the placement and arrangement of the graves ranged around the family monument is final testament to the immutability of sibling relationships, the unchanging nature of family roles. As the eldest of three brothers, Uncle Doc occupies the choicest real estate—his plot overlooks the brook that bubbles merrily along the edge of the cemetery grounds. My father was the youngest—his grave fronts on the road. And Uncle Bill, the middle child, is wedged between them;

147

making peace in the afterlife, no doubt, the way he always did in this one.

In fact he was the first of the brothers to die, and by rights should have had the best gravesite. But there was no question of upsetting even in death the hierarchy determined by birth order and long since assented to. Except by my mother, who resented that her final resting-place, too, would face the highway, as the wives' plots are lined up at the feet of their husbands', a layout determined when the "boys" purchased the family plot. For three decades my mother lobbied for a better location; she wanted to be able to hear the rushing water, she said. The "boys" just laughed. Uncle Doc, who thought she talked entirely too much anyway, used to say she'd be running off at the mouth even in her grave, so she wouldn't be able to hear the brook in the first place.

The wives adopted their husbands' fraternal order of rank in much the same way they took their names. Thus Aunt Lily was the senior wife, my mother the junior, and Aunt Bess the middle. On all whole-family occasions the rules and roles were as defined for the women as they were for the men. Aunt Lily was the boss, which was reason enough for my mother, an eldest child and a real control freak besides, to dispute everything she ordained, from where we had the Passover seder to what the family should give to a distant relative celebrating a wedding or bar mitzvah. Aunt Bess was the mediator in the frequent quarrels between my mother and Aunt Lily; fortunately Bess was born a middle child and so came by her skill naturally. Of the six, Aunt Bess is the only survivor, and she still mediates. When my sister and I quarrel, we complain to Aunt Bess, who gets on the telephone from Florida as soon as the rates go down and scolds us with the litany of our childhood: "You can fight with anybody, but with family you've got to make up."

And I do, or my sister does, because both of us long ago learned that was a major Life Rule. It's one of the values that shaped most of the women of our generation, and we have tried to instill it in our children. But in this, as in so many other areas, we are once again caught in a double bind. We were taught that family is more important than the individual, yet we have lived through a revolution in personal psychology that challenged and deconstructed that notion, and lived through changes in society and the culture that redefined family altogether. The togetherness of the fifties gave way to the self-actualization of the sixties and seventies, when many of us reevaluated our relationships with our families of origin, including our siblings. Some of us went to great distances to assert our independence from them, particularly if we harbored resentments from childhood. Often it took the illness or death of our parents for us to reconcile our differences and value our connection; almost as often such a crisis only exacerbated those differences and nourished our grievances. We may still be influenced by old patterns of sibling rivalry, but we don't want our children to be. Regardless of whether our own sibling bonds are strong or weak, positive or negative, we want our children to love each other, to support each other, and especially to be there for each other when we no longer are. And in the meantime we'd be delighted if just once we could get through Thanksgiving dinner without a major fight.

"I have this idea that the world is so uncertain, they need to be able to count on family more than we did. Wives and husbands come and go, friends disappear, but brothers and sisters are forever. I tell my son, 'I don't care if you disapprove of the way your sister lives, she's still your sister. And if she needed you, I would expect you to help her.' "

"My daughters don't get along, never have. I think when Ben and I are gone, they'll never see each other again, and it makes me very sad. I keep thinking there's something I could be doing to change things between them, because of course I think there's something I did that caused it. Both of them think I loved the other one more."

Unresolved sibling rivalries may be one reason our kids aren't as close as we would like them to be. Family roles established in childhood may be irksome or inappropriate when siblings interact as grown-ups. Siblings often have different expectations about what constitutes being a good sister or brother. And many siblings may have grown into people with different beliefs, lifestyles, attitudes, and interests. Away from parental control, often living far from each other, and not suffering any apparent distress because of the absence of intimacy between or among them, little connects them except us. We can't make them like each other. We can't make them love each other. We can only try to stay out of the middle, love them separately, avoid taking sides, assigning blame, or wallowing in guilt. It can be difficult, especially when we see them acting out unresolved childhood sibling rivalries in their adult interactions, not only with each other but also with their mates, friends, co-workers, or even their own and each other's children. And when they behave toward each other in ways that fall short of our standards, we feel disappointed, angry, and guilty.

My own children have been at odds with each other since they were young. In their twenties, finally, they seemed to have put their old rivalries behind them. Or at least I thought they had.

Jenny had been home for a weekend with her brand-new fiancé; we celebrated their engagement together with my son, Cameron, and his wife. I felt rich in family, warmed by the presence of my children, happy for their happiness, until a few days later when Cameron dropped by after work. There was something on his mind, he said, something that had been troubling him since the weekend. It was minor and petty, and he wasn't proud of it, but he was jealous of a gift I'd made to his sister. In his reckoning she got something he didn't. And it bugged him. He went on to recount other, past sins of unfairness; all of them, he assured me, perfectly understandable, given the circumstances at the time, but still they caused him pain and resentment. And I have always urged him to share his feelings, haven't I?

It took twenty-six years for him to do that, and frankly I'd just as soon he hadn't bothered. Because what he was really telling me was that he felt shortchanged as a child, that she got more of my love and affection than he did. And what happened over the weekend, two decades later, re-stimulated that old pain.

I started to tell him about my efforts to redress the balance of resources I've expended on both of them over the years; yes, I bought her a car, but I gave you a down payment for your house. Yes, there was that last-minute junket to Bermuda with her, but you and I went to Africa for a month and she didn't. And then I shut up. Because it really doesn't matter what I think, or what my truth was. He's interpreted the past in a way I can't change. It's his truth, his story, and he's sticking to it: I loved her more.

So I did what I'd just written one should do, in situations like this. I accepted his version of his past, apologized for my inability to prevent it from happening, and expressed my regret that it caused him pain. Which effectively closed it for him; he felt much better, he said. But it caused me to

think about what might have happened if we'd both han-
dled his resentment differently. If he hadn't told me . . . if I
hadn't listened . . . if I'd been too busy defending myself,
denying his truth, insisting on my own version of events,
and arguing about the details. That's what I've done in the
past, and clearly it hasn't worked, because the argument
keeps resurfacing, the accusations are replayed, the anger
and resentment added to the ledgers both of them keep in
their hearts.

Equity is the ground on which sibling rivalries, in childhood or adulthood, are born and flourish. The disputes over
how we allocate our resources among them are about
whether we loved them equally. But there are other, more
subtle struggles going on among our children. These have
to do with roles, definitions, talents, and territory inherited
and established long ago, and the influence of brothers and
sisters in the development of one's individual as well as
family identity.

YOU ALWAYS LOVED THE OTHER ONE MORE

Regardless of what precipitates in our grown children a
flare-up of childhood rivalry, the root cause is always the
same. Money, gifts, time, attention, interest—they're all
symbols of parental preference. Even when a sensible case
can be made for why we acted as we did, or why we still
do—she's sick, she needed more, you have a job, he

doesn't, and so on—and even when they seem to understand and accept our logic, the hurts of the inner child are not healed but restimulated. This is not only painful for them but shameful; they feel they should have outgrown those feelings by now. And so do we.

As far as our eldest children are concerned, our real crime was having others. Some of them have never forgiven us. Not only were they rudely ejected from their roles as the exclusive objects of our love and attention, they were expected to share the booty with the interlopers. Our middle children suffered not only the jealousy and resentment of siblings on both sides but had constantly to recalibrate how much of our love they were getting compared with what the others in the family received. And our youngest, no matter how indulged or spoiled they were by parents or siblings, dealt from the beginning in an economy of scarcity rather than abundance; they got the leftovers, whatever wasn't used up or spoken for already.

While we were the real culprits—the ones who held the goodies—our children's struggles were waged not with us but with each other. It was safer to blame brothers and sisters for usurping our love or attention than to confront us. And it still is. Much of what happens between parents and children is displaced by them onto their siblings, even though they did not cause the narcissistic injury and are not to blame.

The fact is that we didn't love our children equally. We

loved them differently, because we were different parents
to each of them, depending on who we were when they
were born, what kind of family environment they were born
into, how much they needed us, and how their traits, characteristics, and personalities jibed or clashed with our own.
We didn't treat them equally either. We treated them differently, for the same reasons. And when we face, feel, and
communicate that to them, two things happen: We confirm
the truth they intuitively know, thus validating their emotional experience, and we provide a context for that experience that frees them to work out their relationships among
one another without our interference.

"Yes, sometimes I loved her more," I told my son. "But
sometimes I loved you more, although you might not have
experienced it that way. You struggled to separate from me
the day you were born. You were extremely independent.
She wasn't; she was a clinger. I felt more competent with
her, because she was my second child, and a girl. But as the
first boy in the family, you were your father's and your
grandmother's favorite. I tried to right that imbalance, so
perhaps I overcompensated. I had to work harder with you;
I gave you more attention, more energy, more concern. I
felt as though she was satisfied with how much I loved her,
whereas you were smothered by it."

It was a difficult conversation, but a necessary one. I
watched him as I spoke. When I was finished, he seemed
relaxed and happy; he was right. He had an explanation

for feelings that had been troubling him for a long time. As an adult and a parent himself, he understood and pardoned me.

We have to accept that our feelings for our children are sometimes unequal in order for them to accept it. We are not always able to live up to our own standard of what is just and equitable in the way we apportion our love, and often we overcompensate for it in ways that exacerbate rather than defuse the sibling rivalries of childhood.

CAN THEY COUNT ON EACH OTHER?

Our sons and daughters are part of a generation that will have more siblings than children. It is likely that as they age, they will have to rely on one another as caregivers. Thus doing whatever we can to further close, supportive, mutually rewarding relationships among them is an important task of postparenthood. To accomplish this we have to take ourselves out of the middle and learn not to take sides. We have to look at how we may be subtly pressuring our children to maintain the roles they played growing up in the family, even if the roles no longer fit, or never did. We need to consider how our expectations of them color theirs of each other, how our own unresolved sibling rivalries are sometimes played out in our relationships with our children, and how theirs influence the way they feel about one another today. And finally we have to realize that even if our children don't have the intimate bonds among them we wish they had, we have not failed in some aspect of our parental role. Our sons and daughters are making their own judgments about relationships—going their independent ways. They have a right to choose those they will be close to, and we can't make those choices for them.

THE ETERNAL TRIANGLE

One of the mine fields in sibling relationships is triangulation. In psychological terms triangulation is a defense employed when the tension between two people is so intense that a third is drawn in to draw some of it off; to be a sounding board, go-between, advocate, or stand-in. In transactional analysis triangulation is expressed by the game called Let's You and Her Fight.

When we talk to one of our children through one or more of our others—when we tell one what we can't, for one reason or another, tell, ask, complain, advise, worry, or feel about another directly—we're triangulating. For instance: "Your sister hasn't called me in weeks." "He's ruining his life by dropping out of college." "Your father is very upset about your brother." "I wish you'd talk to her about her weight." "I was really upset when he forgot my birthday." "Don't tell him I'm loaning you this money."

Of course our children do this too: "I don't know why you always give in to him." "That guy is such a loser. If she knew the things I do, she'd drop him." "You let her boss me around." "I think she has a real problem with her two-year-old." "How can you stand it when she takes advantage of you?"

It's not only parent-child and intersibling communication that gets triangulated; many couples form the habit, early in the family, of talking to each other through their children. If it isn't through them, it's often around or about them. And when the children leave home, they are often left with nothing to say to each other or no way to say it.

When you pay your child the compliment of direct interaction instead of triangulated communication, you create intimacy that neither excludes nor divides your other children. You avoid compromising their sibling loyalties or forcing them to choose between their parents and their siblings.

DIVIDED LOYALTIES

"My middle child and I have been extremely close all her life. After my divorce, she became my confidante. In a way she was like a coparent. It wasn't that the others elected her as the emissary to me. They just saw that I listened to her, so when they wanted something, they went through her to get it. And when I had problems with the other ones, I guess I talked them over with her. A few years ago, after she'd been in therapy for a while, she made a conscious attempt to

change our relationship. She said, 'I have to draw some boundaries, Mom. You can't talk to me about the other kids anymore. You're going to die someday, and I want to have a real bond with them, and right now they don't trust me because I'm your confidante. So if you have stuff you need to work out with them, do it directly.'"

Although we want our children to be friends, when they are, we sometimes feel excluded. When the child to whom Kathleen felt closest invited her sister for dinner and didn't ask Kathleen, "I sulked for a week!" When Mavis's son and his wife had marital troubles, and he shared them with his sisters but not with her, she felt shut out, even when her daughter rightly pointed out that Mavis, who never liked her daughter-in-law, couldn't offer her son the more objective advice he got from his sisters.

Sometimes we sabotage our kids' relationships with each other without realizing we're doing so. Frequently this happens when we use one of our children to find out something about another: "Has your sister found a boyfriend yet?" "Has your brother asked you for money?" "Do you know where he spent the weekend?" "Why doesn't she ever talk to me?"

The truth is that children keep secrets from us for our protection or theirs. We wouldn't ask their friends to divulge their confidences, but we're not nearly as careful or discreet in the way we expect their siblings to, even though asking one to spill the beans puts that person in a difficult spot. And once we have the information, we can't act on it without revealing the source, which further complicates and obstructs their relationships.

GETTING OUT OF THE WAY

Despite our good intentions, we may still be intervening in our children's relationships with each other the way we did when they were young. We need to learn to get out of their way and let them deal with one another as individual adults, with their own vision of who their siblings are, which may often be clearer than our own. They interact with each other in the larger world as peers or near-peers; they make their judgments based on wider experience and different norms, and their perceptions are often less clouded by sentimentality than ours. They may also have suffered sibling abuse of which we have been blissfully unaware; they have scores to settle or grievances to redress, and they can't do this when we're in the middle.

We can also get out of their way by allowing them to renegotiate the roles we assigned them when they were younger in ways that are more appropriate to the adults they have become. The circumstances of their lives may be very different now, and they may be unwilling to maintain roles they used to play. This is especially true if they resented those roles then or were resented by their siblings because of those roles.

They may also feel constricted and robbed of any real choice about how they relate to their brothers and sisters today. The child who always took care of the others may have grown into an adult with other demands or fewer resources or less time to expend on her siblings. The baby of the family may have become a respected, accomplished grown-up to whom outsiders look for leadership. It is enormously frustrating to be stuck in roles that don't fit, to be seen as who one was rather than who one has become. When we perpetuate a grown child's outdated role, so do his siblings.

Our children may need our help and/or permission to discard roles that no longer fit them and to renegotiate their sibling relationships. We make it harder for them to forge realistic adult relationships with each other if we hold on to the categories or comparisons of their childhood—she's the brain, he's the shiftless one, this one's the difficult child, that one's the whiz kid. If we persist in looking to the middle child to mediate, the oldest to dominate, the caretaker to help the others even when he or she is already overburdened with other responsibilities. If we expect Lazy won't ever clear his stuff out of the basement, and ask Organized to nag him into it or do it for him. If we give Thrifty control of a trust we've set up for Spendthrift.

"My son has always been the responsible one in the family. All the other kids turn to him when they're in trouble, and he always helps out. But my daughter has really taken

161

advantage of him. She moved in with him and his wife, she borrows money constantly, she keeps making him bail her out of trouble. The others don't help because they know he will, and we can't afford to. It wasn't until my daughter-in-law came to me and said, 'When are you going to let him off the hook?' that I realized how we've all participated in this. My son's business is hurting, he has a sick child of his own, and the other kids are much more able to help—especially Sara, the youngest, who's a substance-abuse counselor. She's the only one who recognized what the real problem with Laura is, and the only one who can really help in this situation, but because she's the baby, no one listened, including me and my husband. The way she's taken over has been a revelation to all of us, and I think Sara's enjoying the new respect she gets from her brothers and sisters."

THE QUASI-PARENT

In large families, especially, there is often pressure on one child—usually the oldest, or the only girl—to take on a parental role with the others. When our children grow up, these quasi-parents find it hard to relinquish that role, even if they find it burdensome or feel taken advantage of by their siblings. They don't want to disappoint us; they feel guilty that they are not living up to our expectations. At the same time they may relish the authority and leadership such a role provides.

We can help the quasi-parents put down their burden by apportioning family responsibilities more equitably, and letting all our children know that what might have been necessary or appropriate years ago is not that way today. Giving grown children tacit or explicit permission to renegotiate sibling responsibilities on their terms, not ours, goes a long way toward defusing sibling rivalries. In turn it allows them to look at how they may be displacing their resentments against their brothers and sisters onto their own spouses, children, and friends by carrying childhood roles into their adult lives.

• • •

To sum up, we have little or no say about whether our children will remain close to and concerned about each other. As adults, they are as free to form relationships with their siblings as anyone else, and shared family history may not be sufficient to keep them together, particularly if their lives, values, and priorities are dissimilar. But often sibling rivalries that last into adulthood get in the way of real connection, which naturally concerns us. We know that this is a generation that may have to count on each other as caretakers, and we want our children to be available to one another when we no longer can be.

When family roles established in childhood but irrelevant or irksome to the adults our kids have become hinder their closeness, we can help by letting go of the identities that accompany their roles. We can set an example by dealing with them as the adults they are, not the fractious or role-defined children they were. We may have guilty feelings about the disproportionate allocation of our attention and affections contributing to their feeling that "You always loved the other one more," but this is not the only source of adult sibling rivalry. Facing, feeling, and communicating to your grown kids your realization that there may be real substance to their sense of having received unequal treatment or love may help release them from the burden of their resentment and make it easier for them to feel close to their siblings. By resisting the temptation to triangulate— to draw one child into our fear, quarrel, or problem with another—and by communicating more directly with each of our children, we also lessen the power of old rivalries to influence their adult relationships. Although we may sometimes feel excluded when they prefer each other's company to ours, they need to do that to tighten their own bonds, to be a family for one another when we're gone. We need to get out of the middle and out of the way, allowing them to renegotiate their roles in the family and with one another. We also need to give the "quasi-parent" permission to set aside a role that may be burdensome.

This isn't to say that we don't want our children to be able to count on each other for sustenance, love, and assistance. But the operative principle here is doing whatever we can to liberate them so that they feel free to decide how, when, and whether to help each other—or, later, to help us.

CHAPTER EIGHT

BONUS BABIES

My grandparents were old when I was born—at least in my memory they are. My father's mother walked heavily with a cane; my mother's father had whiskers sprouting from his ears. They spoke a language I didn't understand, their houses smelled of camphor and cabbage; they were not sophisticated or worldly, even by the standards of their time; and they were frail—a few hours in our boisterous presence was all they could manage.

By contrast, when my children were young, my parents

were healthy, vigorous, lively middle-agers. Every June they sent the plane tickets, and the kids decamped to a house almost as familiar as their own, where for an entire summer they were cherished, indulged, and fully the center of their grandparents' affections and attention.

From my perspective that was a mixed blessing. Yes, the children were safe and well cared for, and I was blissfully free from the stresses and demands of being a working mother. But for weeks after they came home, they were impossible. They couldn't understand why I wouldn't drop everything to play Candyland with them. They were genuinely amazed that I expected them to pick up after themselves. They'd completely forgotten that you don't eat dessert until you finish your vegetables. And they hadn't heard the word *no* for so long that I might well have been speaking a foreign language.

In reality it was a small price to pay. For what they got out of those summers, and a quarter century of their grandparents' love, was something they couldn't get anywhere else: total, unquestioning, uncritical acceptance and adoration. And that was just for starters. Only a grandmother shops for children all year long from the Neiman Marcus Christmas catalog.

After my first child was born, I blamed my labile emotional state on my hormones; there couldn't be any other excuse for being jealous of my own baby. Still, it was nice to feel, finally, that I had done something my parents fully approved of. So when I became a grandmother myself, I took particular pains to make sure the new parents didn't feel neglected. Everyone else brought gifts for the baby—I brought them for the parents. Everyone else rushed to the nursery first—I listened to the contraction-by-contraction recounting of the labor twice before I even peeked. Everyone else deluged the new mother with advice—I didn't offer a morsel. And all that lasted about ten minutes. Since then I have been a walking, talking cliché of a grandmother. And if my kids are jealous, they'll just have to live with it.

Unlike some of my friends, I was in no hurry for my kids to have children. As it turned out, they did it without asking me and under conditions I thought less than optimum. But none of what had seemed so important before the birth mattered the first time I beheld my grandchild and traced with my fingers the tiny face that looked so much like his father's. I decided then that I would create my own relationship with him and maintain it no matter what—I had heard too many unhappy stories about children lost to their grandparents when their own parents separated. And while it has sometimes required making my way through a mine field of conflicting loyalties, I have.

When our children have children, the entire constellation of family relationships shifts. We take on new roles and additional identities that sometimes conflict with our old ones. Life becomes infinitely more complex, responsibilities are reshuffled, needs and priorities change. While most of our attention is focused on the baby, we may not notice how his arrival has altered our perceptions of our children, our spouses, and ourselves.

In the best of cases our grandchildren will be raised in safe, secure, loving circumstances, with two parents who are equally committed to their well-being. We will have the opportunity but not the obligation to participate in their lives, the joy but not the responsibility of caring for them, the luxury but not the necessity of helping secure their future. And we will have the pleasure of seeing our children raise theirs at least as well as we did—even better, if our fondest dreams are realized.

But these days many of us are getting more, and less, than we hoped. Often our children are coming home with theirs—not for a visit but for good. Or they're divorcing, disappearing, and taking our grandchildren with them. Some don't want any help at all; others expect it to be unlimited and are bitter and dismayed when it isn't. Because our life always revolved around them, they believe it should now revolve around their children, even if we've filled up the spaces left by their departure with work, friends, travel, or simply self-indulgence. Today's grandmothers aren't always over the river and through the woods. They're at the gym, at the office, across the continent, or on the road, and doing all the things they promised themselves they'd do when the children were grown. They love their grandchildren and look for ways to show it, opportunities to make a difference in their lives, chances to give them the benefit of their experience, wisdom, and love. But in the final analysis, as one woman, grandmother of three, said, "They aren't the main course, they're the dessert."

WHY NO WOMAN IS EVER TOO YOUNG TO BE A GRANDMOTHER

Nothing makes you realize that your baby isn't your baby any longer so much as her baby. In case you've ignored every other indication that your child is no longer your responsibility, the one he's just taken on will do it. No matter how fit, firm, or even far from fifty you may be, how young in heart, mind, and body you and everyone else thinks you are, becoming a grandmother will knock your sense of yourself as a sexy, desirable woman into a cocked hat, at least for a while.

But whatever sense of loss you feel—and make no mistake, that's what it is—is soon gone. It's replaced by a rush of emotions very like those that overwhelmed you at the birth of your own child: love, pride, amazement, and a sense of arrival; this is why I exist, this is what it's all about, this is the meaning of life. What you don't feel, though, is what has just turned your child from a person into a parent—responsibility. Which is why, after a mercifully brief period of depression during which you wait at intersections for a Boy Scout to help you across the street, wonder whether something you're wearing is too youthful, and finally admit you're too tired for sex, you seem to be your old self once more, only better—more playful, spontaneous, and enthusiastic. You have new reserves of patience, strength, and energy. Your memory improves immediately; you remember every line of nursery rhymes. The worry lines carved into your face by your children disappear without the intercession of a plastic surgeon. Contrary to every expectation, especially your own, you feel young again. There is no better antiaging tonic than grandparenthood, and that's the truth.

There are more grandparents alive today than at any time in history. We are young enough to be a real part of our grandchildren's lives, to watch them grow up, to share our experience with them and teach them what we've learned in our own struggles to reconcile two, often conflicting sets of values. We are affluent enough to help them, powerful enough in numbers alone to demand that government and society respond to their needs, available enough to be there for them when their parents can't be, and aware enough of what worked and what didn't with our own children to be more effective and nurturing with theirs. Our daughters are stressed in ways we weren't—most of them won't have a choice about whether or not to stay home with the children. Our sons are dealing with pressures our husbands didn't face—not just economic but emotional, as their wives rightly demand that their husbands participate equally in parenthood. The more we share what we have and know with them, the stronger their families will be and the safer we make our grandchildren's welfare and happiness. The lines are often difficult to discern between speaking up when we have something constructive to offer—assistance, advice, or the solution to a problem that we can see and they can't—and interfering in our children's right to raise their children as they see fit. Sometimes we don't know where the lines are until we've tripped over them. A useful rule of thumb for the parents of new parents is this: If it's something they'd do themselves if they could, do it. If it's not, don't.

THEY ALL THINK THEY'RE RAISING THE DALAI LAMA

In some ways our children are more like our parents than we are. Life having come full circle, our daughters are as fully invested in professional parenting in the nineties as our mothers were in the fifties, but they bring to their new role the standards and expectations of actual professional experience. They have been in the workplace and know how to establish goals and objectives, complete essential tasks within an allotted time, and manage people. None of that will be of any use to them as parents, particularly once they discover that children have a tendency to grow their own ways. That will frustrate them more than it did our mothers, who had no comparative experience outside the home, and more than it did us; we may not have thrown out the rule books entirely, but as the whole culture grew more permissive, so did the way we raised our children. We can help by reminding them occasionally that no child was ever graduated from college wearing diapers and by pointing out that in spite of our hopelessly old-fashioned notions about raising children, they turned out okay and will certainly remedy any mistakes we made in raising their own. However, there is very little we can or should do to counteract their belief that their child is unique and exceptional, not to mention divine, especially since they are undoubtedly right.

On other issues, however, we will probably disagree. Managing those disagreements is a key task of grandparenthood. While the obvious fact is that our children have the last word, they are more likely to take ours if we offer it in a way they can hear, if we avoid the implication that we are criticizing them, and if we support their decisions. Some of the issues are symbolic and speak to our children's needs to assert their independence; others are content-based, and reflect their own values and philosophy. Your kids may feel strongly about what their children eat, the kind of toys they play with, their religious instruction, how they are disciplined, even whether they're picked up and soothed when they cry. It helps to familiarize yourself with the child-raising theory and technique on which their parenting style is based and try to avoid obvious departures from the rules. But no one really expects you to ignore what experience has taught you is effective. What grandparents have to offer is commonsense wisdom, practical suggestions, and a storehouse of mistakes we've learned from. We've been exposed to a number of parenting theories and techniques and have had wide enough experience with various methods and models to have a pretty good idea of what works in helping children develop confidence, competence, and self-esteem.

IN LOCO PARENTIS

One of the common errors grandparents make is assuming that their child's child is their own. It's an easy trap to fall into, especially in the first fine, careless rapture of nuzzling a newborn; it's almost like being given a second chance at parenthood. And when new parents are anxious, insecure, and exhausted, they may be more than willing to let us take over for them. But a couple of weeks of rising at three A.M. to walk the floor with a wailing infant or a day of chasing a two-year-old around the house is usually enough to teach us the wisdom of nature's original plan; young mothers for young babies. Although circumstances may place us *in loco parentis* for a time, most of our children want to raise theirs themselves. So it's important to support their decisions, back up their authority, and back off when

173

they tell us to, even when we're convinced we know better. We can make rules in our family but not in theirs. We owe our children the right to make their own mistakes with their own offspring—we had our chance with ours. We also need to understand that our grandchildren aren't just our children's children; they're somebody else's too. The way your son or daughter raises, teaches, or disciplines his or her child is the result of an agreement between two people, and you're not one of them. Taking over your child's role as a parent infantilizes him, making him a child again, in his eyes as well as in his offspring's. Undermining your child's authority with his or her children is a zero-sum game; you create conflict for your grandchildren, problems between their parents, and anger in your child. If you insist on doing it your way, regardless of whether it's their way, or even the right way, you'll soon lose the opportunity to do it any way at all.

No matter how old children are, they sense and respond to family conflict. When they see their parents and grandparents fighting over them or things that concern them, their loyalties are divided—they feel caught in the middle. And they blame themselves, not us or their parents, for the trouble in the family.

Intragenerational squabbling over grandchildren is particularly acute when we undermine our children's self-confidence as parents. That happens most often in families when parents are accepting financial or child-care help from grandparents. According to Dr. Helene Kivert, an associate professor of social work at the University of Minnesota, who studies the interactions between generations, "When people get more angry rather than less angry over trivial issues, it's often because they're feeling out of control on other important issues in their lives. At the extremes the parents may feel obliged to yield to the grandparents' requests, or to rebel as if they were adolescents making a show of their independence. The ensuing battles become matters of principle instead of shared attempts to instruct the parents."

"I was separated from my husband for a year when my children were toddlers, and lived at home with them and my parents. My mother and I argued constantly over everything from the kids' bedtime to what they ate; I was so aggravated, I began having migraines again. Then my four-year-old had a siege of severe intestinal problems—vomiting and diarrhea. The pediatrician, who had been my own doctor when I was a child and knew our family well, put his finger on it; he said, 'You and your mother are making your kid sick.' "

We may be footing some of the bills for the grandchildren, but that does not give us the right to call the shots. We can be more supportive of our financially or emotionally strapped children by backing them up, not taking over for them; by respecting their independence as parents, not treating them once again as children.

PICK UP YOUR TOYS AND GO HOME

One decided advantage grandparents have over parents is that our role is strictly optional. Which means that if we don't like the way our grandchildren behave, we can always pick up our toys and leave—or tell them to do the same. We can choose to gift our grandchildren with our attention, while their parents can't. This is an extremely effective position to be in, particularly when all other attempts to discipline the little darlings fail. While love is unconditional, approval isn't. We can demand good behavior and withdraw if we don't get it. We can provide neutral and consistent discipline because we are free from distractions and don't have as great an investment as parents do in its outcome. We can refuse to own a child's behavioral problems and can let them belong to him. We can help children develop a conscience without burdening them with guilt. We can avoid the triangulation that often takes place when children play one parent against another. Because we are not plagued as most parents are by anxiety, self-doubt, and confusion, we can offer our grandchildren a calm, logical adult presence, a loving respite from the crucible of the immediate family. When they are typecast or assigned roles in the family, as they inevitably will be, we can modify or limit the influence of such classification by letting them know we see them as unique individuals with other attributes and characteristics.

"One of my children was slow, dreamy, and not much of a performer academically; the other was born fast forward, a truly gifted kid. I think Billy tended to get lost in the comparing game parents can't help playing. If it hadn't been for his grandmother, who recognized Billy's dreaminess as the true creativity it was and encouraged him, he probably would have been typecast forever as the dumb one. She made us get him tested, find the right school program for him, and let him use her garage for his science experiments. When he won a Westinghouse scholarship, the first person he called to tell about it was her."

HOW NOT TO GET CAUGHT IN THE CROSSFIRE

Grandparents can be a child's best friend when his parents divorce—and must be. Often we are the only source of stability for youngsters whose personal world is falling apart. Although our natural tendency is to ally ourselves with our own offspring, we compromise our opportunity to help a grandchild when we openly take sides, blame, or criticize one or both of the parents. What our grandchildren need from us is reassurance that they will not be abandoned, that they are not the cause of their parents' problems, and that they cannot solve them. What our children need is support for their efforts to rebuild their lives, even if we disagree with their decision to end the marriage. We can't know the pressures and problems they've experienced. Reinforcing their feeling of failure with repeated *If only*s or *I told you so*s will only make them withdraw from us, often taking our grandchildren with them. Sometimes, in spite of our efforts, divorce separates us from our grandchildren, but these days our more militant generation is not accepting that without a fight, even if it means going to court to assert our rights as grandparents. Some parents are concerned that their ex-in-laws will try to kidnap their children; others attempt to punish their former spouses by denying grandparent visitation. And some simply don't want us in their lives, or their children's, any longer. In many states, however, the law recognizes that we have a unique and special bond with the children of our offspring, a right recently upheld by the Supreme Court, and in all fifty states there are laws permitting us to petition the court for visitation under varying circumstances. The Grandparents Rights Organization, a national support group, is lobbying for uniform visitation rights in all states; meanwhile its members offer counseling, advice, and legal assistance to parents who have been cut off from their children's children. *"He had his lawyers and she had hers. When I saw that she was trying to punish him by denying me access to Bobby, I got my own,"* said a woman, whose former daughter-in-law refused to allow her to see her grandson. The child now spends two weeks a year with this woman, who had to defend herself against charges that, if granted visitation, she would insult, defame, and blame her daughter-in-law, thus damaging the parent-child relationship and causing the child serious emotional harm. *"When my son was in the midst of the divorce, I guess I did that, but, as the judge pointed out, all I was doing was re-creating for Bobby the same conflicts caused by the divorce itself. When I realized that, I was able to curb my tongue. And in fact I've come to admire my ex-daughter-in-law. She took on a difficult role and needs all the help she can get."*

Even when both parents agree that grandparents have rights and shouldn't be denied them, the new life arrangements our children make after divorce sometimes limit our access to their children, especially when our child is the noncustodial parent: *"My son and daughter are both divorced. I see her kids much more often than I see his. He and his kids have so little time together, I don't want to intrude on it, and now that his ex-wife has remarried, she doesn't want me around. Still, I call and write as often as I can and have made an effort to stay on her good side. My grandchildren know that I am their advocate, that I will be there for them regardless of what happens in their parents' lives."*

Some grandparents have to contend not only with the animosity of their former son- or daughter-in-law but also with their own children's withdrawal from their children after a bitter divorce: *"My son's lack of interest in his children's welfare after he and his wife split up disappointed me terribly. What made it especially hard was seeing history repeat itself—it was just what his own father did after our divorce. I was determined not to lose my grandchildren and not to let my ex-daughter-in-law punish me for my son's sins. It took a lot of work, but I did it, despite his disapproval. I finally said to him, 'You can make your own decisions about your kids, and so can I, but it's heartbreaking when my grandchildren ask me why their father doesn't love them.' I keep hoping that by maintaining my relationship with them, I leave the door open for him to come around one of these days and resurrect his own."*

Said another woman, *"When my son refused to pay child support, we did it for him. His feeling was that he wasn't going to subsidize his ex-wife's extravagant lifestyle, and he has a point—she spends money like crazy. But we have paid for many of the things the children need that she can't afford—their school fees, braces, and some medical bills. We have told him that we are deducting it from what we will eventually leave him. He's very angry at us. Still, as my husband said, we cannot and will not condone his avoidance of his responsibility when it comes to our grandchildren."*

PLASTIC-COATED GRANDMA

One of life's great pleasures is spoiling a grandchild. After all, why else would they make hand-tucked, have-to-be-hand-washed-and-ironed dresses in sizes 2 to 4x, or leather jackets for the kindergarten set? And while I would never dream of counseling moderation, about which I generally feel as Thomas Aquinas did about chastity (yes, but not yet), it is sometimes worthwhile to consider whether your gift will make your own child's life harder (a set of snare drums or a puppy, for instance) or undermine or contravene parental authority (piercing the Princess's ears or giving a teenage grandson his own car). Be aware that your gifts may remind your children of issues from their childhood that still cause them pain. No matter how innocent of conscious intention you are, it's unwise to comment to a daughter who spent her subteen years in Chubby sizes that "It's such fun to shop for Tiffany because everything looks wonderful on her." It's not particularly tactful to say "It's great to have a kid who knows which end of a baseball bat is up," to a son who was a klutz as a child. Understand, too, that your children have pride; it's important for them to feel as if they're taking care of the necessities and you're only supplying the luxuries, even if that may not be entirely true.

You may be tempted to test whether it's you or your

presents that matter by arriving from time to time without a thing in your luggage for your grandchild. It may even be a strategy agreed upon in advance of your visit by you and your children to teach the grandchildren that it's the thought, not the gift, that counts. There are grandparents who do this. There are very few who do it twice. As Lois Wyse says, there's not a grandmother worth her MBA (Major Buyer Award) who confuses her presents with her presence.

BOON COMPANIONS

To sum up, there are more grandparents alive today than at any time in history. We are young and strong enough to be a real influence in the lives of our grandchildren and to help our children as they struggle with the most difficult job of their lives. But it is their job, not ours, and we need to guard against infantilizing them, compromising their independence, and undermining their confidence in themselves as parents. A good rule to follow is this: If it's something your kids would do for or give to their children, offer to do it or give it. If it's not, don't. When grandchildren get caught in intragenerational struggles, their loyalties are divided, and they react the same way they do when their parents divorce; they feel that it is their fault. And often the issue over which you and your children are quarreling, vis-à-vis the grandchildren, is symbolic, not actual. It has to do with your

relationship with your child, not what's best for your grandchild. Managing disputes with your children is a key task of
grandparenting; making an effort to understand and discuss
philosophical as well as actual theories and techniques of
parenting with them will indicate that you accept their
authority, respect their wishes, and want to act with them as
one consistent voice in matters pertaining to your grandchildren.

The advantage grandparents have over parents is that our
role is volitional; when the little ones don't behave, we can
withdraw from them and allow their behavioral problems to
be theirs, not ours. We are able to see over and beyond the
roles by which they may be typecast in their family, and we
can encourage in them the development of skills and abilities their parents may have overlooked.

When their parents divorce, we can be our grandchildren's best friends—and must be. We need to avoid
taking sides, blaming or criticizing their parents, because
that puts undue stress on their loyalties. If our children or
their former spouses don't want us in their kids' lives any
longer, we can turn to groups like the Grandparents Rights
Organization for legal assistance in securing our right to
remain part of our grandchildren's lives. But even without a
legal struggle it may be difficult to maintain connection
with them, particularly if the custodial parent has moved,
remarried, or is unable to reconcile our needs with his or
hers, or those of the grandchildren.

THE BEST PART

The neat thing about grandchildren is having someone around to make you a child again. Seeing the world through the eyes of a child renews your appreciation for the wonders of nature, the excitement of discovery, the joy of learning. Because we were young, relatively speaking, when our grandchildren were born, we are able to reach out across two generations and find more in common with them than our grandparents could with us. Our job isn't to teach them or guide them or turn them into responsible young people—that's our avocation. Our job is to open their eyes, to expand their horizons, which usually expands ours as well. I've been with skip-generation relations in all sorts of places—on dive boats, in Europe, at the theater, on cruises through the fjords of Scandinavia. I've seen adolescents who wouldn't dream of being caught dead with their parents on a Saturday night happily munching popcorn in movies with Grandpa and Grandma. I've been to political demonstrations, rock concerts, and ball games and watched oldsters and youngsters share their passions and pleasures with one another. I've seen kids cut their hair, change their clothes, and mind their manners to please their grandparents, even when they wouldn't for their parents. "You know why I like you, Grandma?" said four-year-old Jonathan yesterday. "Why?" I asked. "Because I don't have to," he said.

Exactly.

CHAPTER NINE

REVERSALS OF FORTUNE

To be a parent to your own parent is an odd reversal of roles for which nothing prepares you. The acceptance as an adult you have sought for so long is finally yours, but you do not want it—not if the cost is their infirmity and helplessness.

The week my father died, my children kept the hospital vigil with me. They did not want to be there. It was summer, school was out, their friends were at camp, at the mall, at the beach. They were restless, fretful, bored, but I paid their complaints no heed; that week I was a daughter first, their mother second. They were there to learn what I was learning, that they would survive when I no longer did. That some time in the future they would wait for my death as I waited for my father's, in a room like that one. And that they would be frightened then, not for me but for themselves.

A decade later we waited again, my children and I, in another room, in the same hospital, my mother comatose, all of us exhausted from the vigil. "Go home now, Mom, and get some sleep," Jenny whispered as the dawn lightened the sky. "I'll be here for her if she wakes up." I wanted to leave, but could not. Weren't there debts still to be settled, attentions yet to be paid? Was not the deathwatch a mother's due, a daughter's duty? Or was there perhaps an example to be set? "When it's your turn, I'll be here too," she whispered, and this time I was not afraid. She had answered the question I dared not ask, that none of us ever dares ask: *Who will be there for us when it's our turn?*

Counting on our children to take care of us when we're old may be risky. Duty doesn't have the same meaning for our children as it had for us, or for our parents. We look at the way society treats the aged and we shudder. I began the interviewing for this book shortly after the appearance of the newspaper stories about the daughter who abandoned her father at a racetrack, all identifying labels cut out of his clothes; it was an anecdote I was to hear over and over again, a story that clearly hit home: *Could this happen to me?* we all wondered.

Probably not. What was particularly unusual about that situation was that it was a daughter who did it. The data suggest that gender is more reliable than any other factor in determining how our children will deal with us when we are old and that if we have daughters, they will probably care for us, albeit grudgingly if we haven't enjoyed a close, loving relationship with them before our decline. If we have sons, though, they are less likely than their sisters to help us if they don't feel loving toward us; affective ties are more reliable than family bonds in predicting whether or not we can count on them for assistance when we need it. Women are society's caregivers. Why else do we say of a man who takes his mother out for a drive once a month or her garbage out once a week, "What a good son," while we take for granted the daughters who are their aging parents' daily mainstays?

We are strong and healthy now, but someday we won't be, and that's what we think about now, that's the scenario we rehearse in the hours when sleep won't come. What we should be thinking about, during the day as well as in the middle of the night, is making a plan for aging well. A plan that involves selfcare as well as care by others, that allows us to be productive, independent, and in control of our lives as long as we can and that acknowledges that accepting help from our grown kids is not a sign that we are incapable of helping ourselves but an indication that they are capable of giving it. It is proof that we have done our job well. And denying them the opportunity to help is stunting their growth.

Having made the transition from a parent-child relationship based on dependency to one based on mutuality, we will not find it easy to accept the reversal of roles that aging inevitably requires. We can make it easier if we establish the ground rules now, if we get the *What if*s out of the way before the contingency plans need to be put into effect. We need to sit down with the experts—lawyers, doctors, estate planners—and map out what we want done. And then we need to sit down with our children and tell them what decisions we have made and why. They will not want to talk about it, but we must insist. It will make their task easier then, and our level of comfort and security stronger now. And after we have dealt with the business of tomorrow, we can get on with the pleasures of today.

HOW CAN YOU SELL THE HOUSE I GREW UP IN?

A house that was too small when the children were growing up is often too big when they're gone. We want to be free—free of memories, maintenance, taxes, fears, or furniture. We want to mark a change in our circumstances—from married to widowed or divorced, from tied down to unfettered, from working to retired—with a change in our lifestyle. We pore over *Metropolitan*

Home and wonder what it would be like to live with art deco instead of colonial. We read the ads for recreational vehicles and think about waving good-bye to the neighbors. After a weekend in the city we come back to the suburbs, where we moved because of the children, and notice that we're the oldest people in the neighborhood. We visit friends in Florida and think it might be wonderful not to buy snow tires this year. We call in a realtor and we think what we could do with the equity we've built up in our houses. And then we tell the children, and all hell breaks loose. "You'll be so cramped in an apartment," they warn. "You won't know a soul in Sun City," they whine. "Where will we come at Christmas?" they whimper.

This is what we tell them when they ask how we can sell the house they grew up in: We say we won't be cramped at all once we get rid of the stuff they didn't take when they left. We tell them we'll make new friends. And we don't even mention that last year they went to his mother and this year they opened our presents in Vail. Because we know that regardless of the fact that they've been living under their own roof for years now, "home" is a state of mind, and once we change ours, they'll change theirs too.

The night before I turned my house over to its new owners, my children and I walked through the empty rooms, remembering. We pictured how they had looked the first time we saw them, recalled the changes we'd made, the changes we'd lived through. We talked about how our lives had been then and how they were now. Jenny left a note for the teenager who would live in her room, warning that those in the kitchen could hear her every word through the heating vent. Cam left a map showing the younger kids the shortcut through the woods to their new school. And finally it was I who had to be dragged away, not they.

CAN TWO WOMEN EVER SHARE A KITCHEN?

When I was a girl, we lived in a neighborhood where every house except ours had at least three generations under one roof. My mother was the only woman whose mother or mother-in-law didn't live with her: "Two women can never share one kitchen," she said, a fact of her life perhaps, but not of everyone's. Some of us manage quite well, particularly when the arrangement is mutual, the parties flexible, the spouses agreeable, and the relationship respectful: *"It works for us because we work at it. I wanted to stay in this house, and I couldn't manage it alone. Also, the market was too depressed to sell. My kids needed more space and a good school district, but they couldn't afford to buy. When they moved in, we remodeled. I have what amounts to my own apartment downstairs, and they have the rest of the house. They don't assume that I'm an unpaid baby-sitter, and I don't expect*

190

them to wait on me. We try to respect each other's privacy, and usually we succeed. When there is friction, we work it out. It is a good partnership."

Another woman moved with her son and his family when they were transferred across the country shortly after she retired. *"I guess I expected to just move into their life as well as their house, and it didn't work. Once I got involved in the new community and made some friends, it was better, but it still wasn't perfect. I found another woman my age in a similar situation, and we took a place together. Sometimes it's easier living with a stranger than it is with family—you try harder."*

Most of us want to stay in our own homes as long as we can; it's part of our sense of security and identity. And we desperately do not want to be a burden to our children. But changes in health, income, and even our neighborhoods may force us to make other arrangements. "I think your kids should be your last resort, not your first," says Vera, who made a careful study of alternative housing possibilities when health problems forced her to retire. She didn't like anything she found, so in the last three years she has shared her home with a succession of college students who shop, cook, and clean for her. Paula and her husband, together with two other couples, are building their own retirement home now, several years before they'll need it—three self-contained living units, shared common areas, and a separate apartment for visiting children and grandchildren: "It'll be a caretaker place at first, because we won't be living there year-round; it's in a vacation community," she says. "But eventually it'll be for a caregiver, someone we'll hire. The six of us have been friends for thirty years, and none of us wants to depend on our kids when we're old."

Well, some of us may have to, whether we like it or not, but planning in advance of need can make the transition easier. Once again, this is something our children won't want to talk about, but we must insist. "We won't make you promise you'll never put us in a home if you'll sit down with us and consider how we're going to handle it when we can no longer manage on our own," Louise and Henry said to their children recently. They developed a number of possibilities ranging from a reverse equity mortgage, which would allow them to stay in their house as long as they wished, to a retirement complex that offers a number of living situations from individual apartments to assisted-care facilities. Their children feel relieved of responsibility, and they feel secure about the next stage of their lives. What prompted their action was the desperate situation they had faced when their own parents fell ill and became incapable of living on their own. They had gained considerable knowledge while trying to find acceptable solutions. Many of us in the "sandwich" generation have had similar experiences and are resolved to plan our own futures while we still can.

ASKING FOR HELP WHEN YOU HAVE TO

There was a time, in our parents' memory if not our own, when people naturally did for each other much of what we pay strangers to do for us now, from shoveling the snow from the front door to listening as we pour out our troubles. Somehow it's easier to put the transaction on a paying basis than call on ties of friendship, family, or community. Also, suggests psychotherapist Marv Thomas, that frees us of the obligation to repay the favor. Asking for help from our children should be easier than asking a stranger, but it isn't, perhaps because we think they should know without asking what it is we need. But unless we tell them, they don't.

"My mother was such a martyr. She was the epitome of those jokes about how many does it take to change a light bulb, never mind, I'll just sit here in the dark. I have made it a habit to ask my kids for help in small ways, just to get them used to the idea that someday I may need it in bigger ways. I asked my daughter to help me find a lawyer when I needed one, and my son to take me shopping for a new car. They look after my plants and my cat when I'm away. I asked my granddaughter to teach me to use a computer, and her brother to program my VCR. They know things I don't, and they have strength and energy I find myself lacking these days. I do plenty of things for them too. After all, what are families for?"

What indeed? Most of us have little experience asking

for help, and less inclination to do so. But if we look at it, as Stevie does, as "the transference of responsibilities and obligations from one generation to the next," it gets easier. And if we are realistic about their willingness and their capabilities, we may never have to depend, like Blanche DuBois in *A Streetcar Named Desire,* on the kindness of strangers.

RITES OF PASSAGE

When children leave home to go on to their own lives, so, sometimes, do we or our spouses. Perhaps we stayed together for the sake of the children, or maybe we didn't notice until they'd left that we had little else in common. Whether we leave or our partner does the leaving, whether it is an amicable divorce or a decidedly unfriendly one, our children, despite their maturity, will be affected. It may not be as obvious or as dramatic as if they were still children, but there is significant emotional weight to a parental divorce no matter what the child's age.

What is different with grown children is their own experience of life and love. Theoretically at least, that should make it easier for them to understand and empathize. It will, once they get over the shock, if we can refrain from demanding that they take sides and can assure them that we will be okay. We must not expect them to accept our new partners, if we have them, as surrogate parents, or our new stepchildren as their siblings. In time they may, but it will be at their inclination, not our insistence.

When parents divorce, the biggest questions young children have are "Is it my fault?" and "What does this mean to my life?" While most adult children know that the answer to the former is no, they are not at all certain of the answer to the latter. They will wonder if they're suddenly going to be saddled with new responsibilities for one or both of their parents and if they're going to be put in the middle between them. They will be concerned with where their loyalties should reside and how the divorce will affect their financial future. They'll ask why we couldn't stay married any longer, or even why we didn't get divorced years ago. And they'll want to know where they'll be expected at Thanksgiving.

While we will assure them that this divorce is our business, not theirs, we may still feel compelled to offer them more of an explanation than we might have when they were younger, simply because they're adults, to talk to them as we would our peers. The best advice on this topic comes from those of us who've been there: Don't. *"Go to a shrink, talk to your friends, discuss it with your pastor or your rabbi, but don't give your kids any more details than you need to. If the reason is obvious—for example if Daddy brings his twenty-five-year-old girlfriend around, or you've been taking separate vacations for years—they'll know it. You're under no obligation to share your most intimate secrets with them, nor should you. Because those secrets will make them uncomfortable, and because you owe a debt of loyalty to their other parent, and to the family you used to be."*

WHEN THE ROLES REVERSE

Actuarially speaking, the chances are that we will out-live our husbands. Some of us already have. We may not be able to be of much help to our children in the immediate aftermath of their father's death, but there will come a time when we are able to share their grief as they have shared our own. This is often a time when grown children begin the process of role reversal; in their eagerness to help, to do for us what our spouses once did, they often attempt to parent us, which can be comforting for a time but irritating after a while.

Our children will often respond to our loneliness by attempting to do for us the things they believe they'd want done for them if they were in our position. We may never complete our mourning, but in time we will get over it. That is the point at which we may want to reassess exactly what it is we want from our children: companionship, assistance with the logistics of living alone, help with our financial affairs, even something as simple as a regular phone call to check and see how we are. Where we get into trouble is not communicating clearly with them what our needs and desires are. Often we let communication lapse until the moment when the pot boils over, when we feel our independence or even our maturity is at risk: *"When Bill died, my kids really stepped into the breach. They took over—they were great. But when I was ready to resume my life, they treated me like I was a child, incapable of making any decisions on my own. They hovered over me until I felt smothered, infantilized. We got quite testy there for a while. I finally had to say to them, 'Look, I appreciate everything you've done, but I have to get used to being on my own sometime, or you'll have me on your hands forever.' "*

The tendency to rely on our children for our sole companionship in old age, and especially after the death of a spouse, is understandable. And most children, acting out of their own love and concern, will do as much for us as we want. But it's important to remember that we still have a life—we still have interests, concerns, work, and pleasures to enjoy alone or with others. Our children are in the middle of their lives while we're approaching the end. While we may have to depend on them for help, we want to avoid burdening them at the expense of their own obligations, responsibilities, and families. And while we may spend a great deal of time lingering in the past, they're not going to be as interested in our yesterdays as they are in their tomorrows.

• • •

To sum up, how much can we count on from our children as we age and are no longer able to manage on our own? This will depend, to some extent, on whether we have sons or daughters and on what the quality of our relationship with them has been. It will also depend on the wishes we communicate to them now, while we are still in command of our faculties, our bodies, and our finances. But it will not be an easy discussion, because our children will resist it.

The role reversal that occurs when children parent their parents can pull families apart, try the patience and stamina of both generations, and strain the closeness and connectedness between them. But it can also strengthen the relationship; it allows our children to express their gratitude to us, their love and affection, in ways they might otherwise not be able to articulate.

The best thing we can do for ourselves and for them is to make a plan for positive aging, well in advance of its happening. This includes making decisions about how matters affecting our health and welfare will be resolved; about financial and estate planning; and about how we want the end of our life to be managed, to the extent that it is within our control or theirs. It may be helpful to include our children in the decision-making process; to discuss our wishes and desires with them, allow them to offer input, and consider how our choices will impact on them. It will be necessary to communicate our decisions, even to put them in writing, so that our wishes can be carried out and our children are relieved of making difficult choices about us without guidance we may not be able to give them.

EPILOGUE

HOW TO TELL THE PARENT FROM THE CHILD

The one who orders the lettuce-leaf salad is the child; the one with the chocolate mousse is the parent.

The one driving the station wagon is the child; the one in the sports car is the parent.

The one buying the training pants is the child; the one buying the little velvet dress is the parent.

The one in the big house in the suburbs is the child; the one in the *pied-à-terre* in the city is the parent.

The one staying home with the kids is the child; the one with the title on the office door is the parent.

The one cooking the turkey is the child; the one picking the mince pies up at the patisserie is the parent.

The one lying down on the sofa is the child; the one playing horsey on the living-room floor is the parent.

The one going to meet the plane from Nepal is the child; the one getting off it is the parent.

The one who's too tired to go dancing is the child; the one who just ran the marathon is the parent.

The one who gets up at dawn is the child; the one who sleeps in until noon is the parent.

The one with the furrowed brow and all the responsibility is the child; the one who's footloose, free, and grinning from ear to ear is the parent.

• • •

In spite of all the propaganda about what a fabulous time of life this time can be for a woman, so far I haven't found too many advantages that I wasn't expecting. For instance I knew it would be great to get senior-citizen discounts when I travel, a relief to be beyond romantic adventures, a pleasure to give up on the gym. As it turns out, they don't give those discounts for scuba-diving or mountain-climbing trips, just for G-rated movies and mah-jongg tournaments. As soon as I gave up on romance, I fell in love with someone who's not even middle-aged yet. And the reason I've let my gym membership lapse isn't because I can't do ten jumping jacks to the music of James Brown any longer but because I just don't have time after riding my new mountain bike twenty miles a day. (It's all on the flat, but who's counting?)

The one thing I never counted on, though—the great gift of this stage of life—is the pleasure, pride, and delight in being a postparent.

For many years our children learn from us. We instruct them in the ways of the world, teach them what's truly important, and offer our experience and wisdom as a guide for them. The best role reversal is when we start learning from them. When we are able to see, hear, and feel things from their perspective. When they put us in touch with a world from which an older generation is often excluded. When we can call on their particular strengths, abilities, and knowledge for help in solving our problems, whether it's carrying our luggage, programming the VCR, or telling us what a man means when he says "Let's have lunch." And when they enrich our lives with their spouses, children, in-laws, and friends.

I have learned so much from my children, their partners, and their children. I remember realizing when my son and daughter were born that they had opened a door in my heart I never otherwise would have known was there. And what happens when they grow up, if you're as lucky as I've been, is that the door in their hearts opens too. You're still their mother, but you're their friend too . . . and they're yours.

A RESOURCE GUIDE FOR THE PARENTS OF GROWN-UP CHILDREN

The groups listed provide local referrals in the private and public sectors for persons of all income brackets. Community agencies such as the Family Service Agency, United Way, Crisis Intervention Service, Mental Health Services and city and county government offices provide information and assistance in a given geographic area. Your family doctor, lawyer, or clergyman may also provide services or referrals, as will the counseling service or student health department of a college or university in which your child is enrolled.

ORGANIZATIONS

Alcoholics Anonymous
Box 459, Grand Central Station
New York NY 10163

American Association of Marriage and Family Counselors
225 Yale Avenue
Claremont, CA 91711.

Federation of Parents and Friends of Lesbians and Gays, Inc.
P.O. Box 24565
Los Angeles, CA 90024

Grandparents'-Children's Rights, Inc.
5728 Bayonne Avenue
Haslett, MI 48850

Grandparents Raising Grandchildren
P.O. Box 104
Colleyville, Texas 76034

Legal Services Corporation
400 Virginia Avenue SW
Washington DC 20024

Narcotics Anonymous
16155 Wyandotte Street
Van Nuys CA 91406

National Alliance for the Mentally Ill/Sibling and
    Adult Children Network
2101 Wilson Boulevard, Suite 302
Arlington VA 22201

National Anorexic Aid Society
5796 Karl Road
Columbus OH 43229

National Association of Alcohol and Drug Abuse Counselors
918 F Street NW, Room 400
Washington DC 20004

National Coalition Against Domestic Violence
2401 Virginia Avenue NW, Suite 306
Washington DC 20037

National Self-Help Clearing House
33 W. 42nd Street
New York NY 10036

HOTLINES

AIDS National Gay/Lesbian Crisis Line   800-221-7044

Alcohol Helpline   800-252-6465

Child Abuse
  Parents Anonymous Hotline   800-532-0386
  Child Help USA   800-422-4453

Drug Abuse
  National Cocaine Hotline   800-262-2463
  National Institute on Drug Abuse   800-638-2045

Grandparents Rights	517-339-8633
Handicapped Crisis Line	800-452-0525
Independent Living Lifeline Systems	800-451-0525
National Abortion Federation	800-638-6725
National Health Information Hotline	800-336-4797

BIBLIOGRAPHY

Aldrich, Robert, and Glenn Austin. *Grandparenting for the
    Nineties*. Escondido, Cal.: Erdmann Publishing, 1991.
Borhek, Mary. *Coming Out to Parents*. Cleveland: Pilgrim
    Press, 1983.
Boston Women's Health Book Collective. *Our Families, Our-
    selves*. Alice Ryerson, Wendy Sanford, editors. New
    York: Random House, 1978.
Boston Women's Health Book Collective. *Ourselves, Grow-
    ing Older*. Paula Brown Doress and Diana Laskin Siegal,
    editors. New York: Simon & Schuster/Touchstone, 1987.
Brans, Jo. *Mother I Have Something To Tell You*. New York:
    Doubleday, 1987.

Erikson, Erik. *Adulthood*. New York: Norton, 1976.

Gilligan, Carol. *In a Different Voice*. Cambridge, Mass.: Harvard University Press, 1982.

Gould, Roger. *Transformations*. New York: Touchstone/Simon & Schuster, 1978.

Greer, Dr. Jane. *Adult Sibling Rivalry*. New York: Crown, 1992.

Haines, James and Margery Neely. *Parents' Work Is Never Done*. Far Hills, N.J.: New Horizon Press, 1989.

Hallowell, Edward, and William Grace. *What Are You Worth?* New York: Weidenfeld & Nicholson, 1989.

Kaplan, Paula. *Don't Blame Mother*. New York: Harper & Row, 1989.

Kegan, Robert. *The Evolving Self: Problems and Process in Human Development*. Cambridge, Mass.: Harvard University Press, 1982.

Klingelhofer, Edwin. *Coping with Your Grown Children*. New York: Dell, 1989.

Littwin, Susan. *The Postponed Generation*. New York: William Morrow, 1986.

Mancini, Jay, editor. *Aging Parents and Adult Children*. Lexington, Mass.: Lexington Books, 1987.

Millman, Marcia. *Warm Hearts, Cold Cash*. New York: Free Press, 1991.

Moorman, Margaret. *My Sister's Keeper*. New York: Norton, 1992.

Okimoto, Jean and Phylis Stegall. *Boomerang Kids*. New York: Pocket Books, 1987.

Rich, Adrienne. *Of Woman Born*. New York: Norton, 1986.

Secunda, Victoria. *When You and Your Mother Can't Be Friends: Resolving the Most Complicated Relationship of Your Life*. New York: Delacorte Press, 1990.

——. *Women and Their Fathers: The Sexual and Romantic Impact of the First Man in Your Life*. New York: Delacorte Press, 1992.

Smith, Shauna L. *Making Peace with Your Adult Children.* New York: Plenum Press, 1991.

Viorst, Judith. *Necessary Losses.* New York: Ballantine, 1986.

White, Jerry and Mary. *When Your Kids Aren't Kids Anymore.* Colorado Springs, Colorado: NavPress, 1991.

Wyse, Lois. *Funny, You Don't Look Like a Grandmother.* New York: Crown Publishing Group, 1988.

INDEX